Timothy D. Hall
Central Michigan University

Anne Hutchinson
Puritan Prophet

THE LIBRARY OF AMERICAN BIOGRAPHY

Edited by Mark C. Carnes

Longman

Boston   Columbus   Indianapolis   New York   San Francisco   Upper Saddle River
Amsterdam   Cape Town   Dubai   London   Madrid   Milan   Munich   Paris   Montréal   Toronto
Delhi   Mexico City   Sao Paulo   Sydney   Hong Kong   Seoul   Singapore   Taipei   Tokyo

Editorial Project Manager: Rob DeGeorge
Editorial Assistant: Amanda Dykstra
Senior Marketing Manager: Maureen
E. Prado Roberts
Senior Marketing Assistant: Ashley Fallon
Operations Specialist: Renata Butera
Cover Designer: Karen Salzbach
Manager, Visual Research: Beth Brenzel
Manager, Rights & Permissions: Zina Arabia
Image Permission Coordinator: Angelique
Sharps
Manager, Cover Visual Research &
Permissions: Karen Sanatar

Cover Illustration: Alethea Hall
Full-Service Project Management: Aparna
Yellai, GGS Higher Education Resources,
a Division of PreMedia Global, Inc.
Composition: GGS Higher Education
Resources, a Division of PreMedia
Global, Inc.

Text Font: Sabon

Credits and acknowledgments borrowed from other sources and reproduced, with permission, in this textbook appear on appropriate page within text.

Library of Congress Cataloging-in-Publication Data
Hall, Timothy D.
   Anne Hutchinson: Puritan prophet/Timothy D. Hall; edited by Mark C. Carnes. — 1st ed.
      p. cm.
   Includes bibliographical references and index.
   ISBN-13: 978-0-321-47621-0
   ISBN-10: 0-321-47621-2
1. Hutchinson, Anne Marbury, 1591–1643. 2. Puritans—Massachusetts—Biography.
3. Women—Massachusetts—Biography. 4. Social reformers—Massachusetts—Biography.
5. Antinomianism. 6. Freedom of religion—Massachusetts. 7. Massachusetts—History—
Colonial period, ca. 1600–1775. 8. Massachusetts--Biography. I. Carnes, Mark C.
(Mark Christopher), 1950- II. Title.
   F67.H92H34 2010
   303.48'4092—dc22
   [B]

                              2009035258

For Alethea

Contents

Editor's Preface   vii

Author's Preface   ix

Chapter 1 Growing Up Puritan in Elizabethan England   1

Chapter 2 Anne Hutchinson and the Church Militant   22

Chapter 3 "A Profitable Member among Us"   43

Chapter 4 Secret Quarrels   62

Chapter 5 Trouble in Churches and Commonwealth   81

Chapter 6 Trial   102

Chapter 7 "A Dayngerus Instrument of the Divell"   123

Epilogue: "The Sainted Anne Hutchinson"   144

Glossary of Terms   152

Study and Discussion Questions   160

A Note on the Sources   166

Index   173

Editor's Preface

We know of Anne Hutchinson chiefly through the trials that caused her to be expelled from her church and cast out of Massachusetts Bay Colony. The surviving records reveal a woman whose reading of the Bible was informed by a penetrating intellect, who expressed her views in clean, sharp words that resonated with the scores of people who flocked to her home, and whose exchanges with the orthodox ministers and with Governor John Winthrop were characterized by a biting wit. Hutchinson was banished in part because she proved to be a formidable opponent.

That Hutchinson was an important figure in early New England is indisputable; but historians differ as to the significance of her life. Some regard her as a free-thinker whose victimization prefigured subsequent instances in American history where entrenched political and social elites suppressed dissidents. Other scholars enshrine Hutchinson as a strong-willed woman whose challenge to patriarchal authorities anticipated the woman suffrage movement and modern feminism.

But biographer Timothy Hall insists on drawing a portrait that Hutchinson herself would have recognized. Though Hutchinson fearlessly contended with powerful colonial officials, she was no free-thinking rebel; and though she delighted in flaunting her intellectual superiority over males who were accustomed to deference, she did not work for the emancipation of women. Hutchinson, Hall shows, was a Puritan prophet, someone who firmly believed that she had received God's free gift of grace and who lived her life in accordance with His wishes—as she discerned them. She came to blows with religious and secular authorities over what God wanted of people.

This dispute may strike modern readers as foolish. How could Christian leaders, ostensibly guided by the precepts of Christ, be so intolerant of Hutchinson's religious opinions? But Hutchinson was equally intolerant of her critics. And that is a key point: Hutchinson lived in an age of theological disputation that may seem far removed from our own preoccupations and concerns. But people at all times and places confront difficult existential dilemmas; and they look to the prophets of their age for guidance and solace. If today's most sought-after prophets discuss our prospects for material well-being, speaking an arcane language of hedge funds, credit default swaps, and sub-prime mortgage derivatives, seventeenth-century Puritans were preoccupied with the prospects of their eternal souls, becoming specialists in theological terms such as sanctification, justification, and Arminianism.

Hall's engaging and provocative biography leads us into a world very different from our own. But who can assert that the Puritan preoccupations were more absurd?

MARK C. CARNES
ANN WHITNEY OLIN PROFESSOR OF HISTORY
BARNARD COLLEGE/COLUMBIA UNIVERSITY

Author's Preface

The story of Anne Hutchinson is deceptively familiar to most who recognize her name. Even those who have forgotten or never heard of her will soon express familiarity when presented with a summary of her life. They have often encountered the theme before—the lone woman standing solitary and defiant against an assembly of men who sit in narrow-minded judgment of her ways. The contours of her tale seem to slip effortlessly into the well-worn grooves of this very modern plot line. For many she is the first American Woman—bold, independent, self confident, articulate, assertive of her rights in the face of those bent on denying them.

Yet when set within its original seventeenth-century context, Hutchinson's tale reveals odd angles and unexpected features which fit poorly with an American script fashioned for her centuries after her death. The assumptions she shared with her contemporaries concerning faith, freedom, gender, and social obligation gave her choices and actions a set of meanings unfamiliar to most modern observers. Those shared assumptions also framed the controversy which erupted over her views as the first generation of colonists in Massachusetts labored to establish a stable society on the edge of a new world charged with possibility and danger.

A study of Hutchinson's life in her own time thus gives us the opportunity to enter a different world and to encounter there a powerful, tragic figure very different from the woman our own assumptions would lead us to expect. Her story also affords a fresh examination of New England's founding generation—its members' purpose in coming to America, the kind of society they hoped to found, and the place envisioned for women and men in that new society. Hutchinson's experience illuminates the apparently fine but crucial differences she and her contemporaries discovered in their religious convictions, as well as the debates over how those convictions should distinguish their New England from the *old* England they left behind.

The story of Massachusetts's founding generation has changed significantly in its telling over the past thirty years. Fresh investigation into all aspects of the English Reformation has yielded a much deeper understanding of the diverse strains of English Protestant thought and practice which shaped the beliefs and practices of Massachusetts Bay's first colonists. Recent analysis of the tensions which wracked England during the 1630s has led to a greater recognition of how quickly the situation on the ground was changing for those thousands of "hotter sort of Protestants" who each year sold their estates and packed their families on sturdy wooden ships bound for a new home three thousand miles across the Atlantic. A greater attention to the transatlantic context of religious developments in New England has contributed to a better awareness of the welter of confusion produced as successive waves of immigrants introduced fresh debates generated by the growing religious conflict at home.

This new scholarship has included significant reassessment of Anne Hutchinson and the Antinomian Controversy. It has permitted a clearer, more nuanced view of how Hutchinson understood herself, what made her such a magnetic agent of divine grace for some of her contemporaries and "so dangerous an instrument of the devil" to others. Her biography provides the reader a glimpse into the world of seventeenth-century Massachusetts Bay from the perspective of a woman who considered herself one of the godly—those English Protestants who had exercised true faith in Jesus, who had experienced genuine forgiveness of their sins, and who devoted themselves to pleasing God through every thought and deed.

Few sources survive concerning Anne Hutchinson's life. She left no letters or diary. Most of what historians know about her comes from the transcripts of two trials—the first before the Massachusetts General Court in November 1637, the second before the congregation of the Boston church in March 1638. A few scraps of information may be gleaned from church records in England and America, several entries in the diary of Massachusetts Governor John Winthrop, and seventeenth-century pamphlets published concerning the controversy. I have therefore organized the chapters of her life story around statements made at her trial which hark back to those periods of her life. Chapters 1 through 6 open with italicized excerpts from the transcript of her civil trial which serve to introduce the chapter's themes.

As in any such undertaking, the author can take only partial credit for this work while bearing full responsibility for its shortcomings. John Hannah first sparked my interest in the puritans almost thirty years ago, Jerald Brauer fanned the flame, and T.H. Breen introduced me to exciting new ways of understanding them within their seventeenth-century world. A summer Calvin Faculty Seminar in Christian Scholarship under the direction of Laura Lunger Knoppers provided my first opportunity to explore Anne Hutchinson and the Antinomian Controversy in depth. A sabbatical from my regular duties at Central Michigan University provided the time needed to launch this project. I am grateful to Mark Carnes for his thoughtful editorial comments throughout. Michael Winship at the University of Georgia generously read through the entire manuscript in meticulous detail and offered many corrections and suggestions for improvement. I owe a great debt to Michael Boezi for his patience with me as this project has progressed by fits and starts, to Vanessa Gennarelli for shepherding much of the first draft, and to Rob DeGeorge for seeing the project through to completion. The book is also much better for the efforts of the following reviewers who gave their time to read the manuscript and offer comments: Kay Blalock, Saint Louis Community College–Meramec; Francis J. Bremer, Millersville University; B.R. Burg, Arizona State University; Robert M. Calhoon, University of North

Carolina–Greensboro; Kelly Lankford, MacMurray College; Marla Miller, University of Massachusetts Amherst; and Caryn E. Neumann, Miami University of Ohio. My daughter Alethea sat patiently though a reading of the first draft and offered ruthless criticism. If the final book is more accessible to my readers, much of the credit belongs to her and to my wife, Sheree. I am grateful to both of them and to my son Ian for their unfailing love, patience, and support.

TIMOTHY D. HALL

Growing Up Puritan in Elizabethan England

"The sentence of the court you hear is that you are banished from out of our jurisdiction as being a woman not fit for our society, and are to be imprisoned till the court shall send you away." The grim words of Massachusetts governor John Winthrop echoed from the plain wooden walls of the Newton village meetinghouse on that cold November day in 1637. The woman before them scanned the faces of her judges, the members of the General Court who flanked the governor. She had endured the North Atlantic passage three years before to join these men in building a community and church dedicated to God's glory. She had worshiped with many of them. She named many of their wives among her friends. She had talked with them, laughed with them, cried with them, and prayed with them. She had assisted at the birth of some of their children. Now, with these words, the court was expelling her from the network of friends and neighbors she had served and grown to love.

Anne Marbury Hutchinson had conducted an often brilliant defense against her accusers for the past two days in an effort to avert this moment. Now she voiced one final question. "I desire to know wherefore I am banished?" she asked. "Say no more," Winthrop replied, "the court knows wherefore and is satisfied."

T he potent scene of this defiant woman, standing alone in the mid-November chill against a wall of the puritan magistrates of Massachusetts, has fired the imaginations of American religious leaders, novelists, and social activists up to the present day. Like a Rorschach ink blot, they interpret her solitary stance as foreshadowing the disorders or aspirations of their own times. Some eighteenth-century New England ministers viewed Hutchinson as a precursor of the religious upheavals of the Great Awakening, which took place one hundred years later. Nineteenth-century novelist Nathaniel Hawthorne described her in highly ambivalent and ironical terms as "the sainted Anne Hutchinson," prophetess of the sentimental womanhood of the Victorian era. In 1920 as the Nineteenth Amendment for women's suffrage neared ratification, the federated Women's Clubs of Massachusetts memorialized Hutchinson as a "courageous exponent of civil liberty and religious toleration." The bronze statue bearing these words still stands on the Massachusetts State House lawn. The cloaked figure, its hand resting protectively on a young girl clinging to its skirts, invites visitors to imagine Hutchinson as a seventeenth-century feminist, a champion of women's rights in her own time, and an inspiration to those who continue that struggle today.

What should we make of this remarkable woman and her tragic fate? How did she understand herself? How did her contemporaries understand her? What in Anne Hutchinson's speech or conduct troubled "the peace of the Commonwealth and the churches" of Massachusetts Bay during the tumultuous events of 1635–1637? What role did gender play in her accusation, trial, and banishment? What role did puritan religion play? What do the actions of the ministers and magistrates reveal about the character of the colony contemporaries labeled the "godly commonwealth?"

Answers to such questions can come only from a thorough examination of Anne Hutchinson's experience within the interplay of religion, culture, and politics in early modern England and its first colonies. Hutchinson's life provides a glimpse into a world of assumptions very different from the present. Seventeenth-century ideas about women, men, and the relationships between them were shifting in subtle ways as Protestant belief entwined with English life during the reign of Queen Elizabeth I (1558–1603). Central to this shift was a new way of thinking about how a person could gain salvation and how that person could know that he or she was truly saved. A wrong answer to this question could jeopardize souls, and puritans agonized and debated intensely over rival responses. The new ideas about salvation also held important implications for how people should conduct themselves in daily life. Through sermons and advice literature, Protestant teachings about various aspects of domestic life came together to form a model of true Protestant womanhood. But here too was ample room for disagreement and debate.

This heady mix of new ideas, expectations, and debates shaped Anne Hutchinson and her conduct as well as that of all her Boston neighbors as they sought to build a model Protestant commonwealth on the shores of Massachusetts Bay. The stakes could scarcely have been greater. Their salvation and that of their children depended on getting the questions of salvation right. So did the harmony of their religious and social life. The success of the colony itself—and with it, the very survival of colonial men, women, and children—depended on their ability to maintain harmony and mutual cooperation. In this highly charged context, Hutchinson's status as a Protestant woman, and the way she used that status to advance her own conclusions about divine grace and salvation, eventually persuaded colonial officials that she was a very dangerous woman.

The controversies which engulfed Anne Marbury Hutchinson in 1637 originated in the Protestant Reformation, a movement which began more than 70 years before her birth. In 1517 an obscure German monk named Martin Luther challenged the Catholic Church's decrees describing how a person could be saved—could receive divine forgiveness for sins, be "justified" or made right with God, and be assured that heaven awaited her or him on the other side of death. Like other humanist scholars of his day, Luther was troubled by the stark contrast between the simple Christianity he found in the pages of the Bible and the elaborate system of hierarchy, ceremony, and ritual in the Church of his own day. He particularly objected to the practice of selling "indulgences," or special pardons said to reduce the time a departed Christian soul had to spend in Purgatory before being admitted to heaven. To Luther, this practice symbolized much that was wrong with the Church of his day. The idea of buying one's way out of punishment seemed to fly in the face of the Bible's declaration that forgiveness was a simple gift of God received by faith, not by observing elaborate rituals or performing good deeds. Indeed, Roman Catholicism's system of ritual duties seemed to Luther to invite hypocrisy by deceiving people into thinking that all they needed was correct observance of rote obligations, not sincere and humble faith in the majestic, living God.

Luther's fame grew rapidly as new print technology spread his ideas. Soon other religious leaders took up the challenge. Most had become impatient with the Church's widely recognized corruption and weary of its many traditions. Many questioned the idea that in the ritual of the Mass, the bread and wine of Communion became the literal body and blood of Jesus. They doubted whether it was right for a true Christian to bow to the Virgin Mary or to ask the saints to pray for them. They were skeptical of the idea that believers needed a priest to act as intermediary between themselves and God, especially the idle, uneducated, gluttonous, and lusty clergy assigned to too many parish churches. Others were excited about the new learning sweeping Northern Europe, especially the prospect of exploring the Bible afresh without the constraints of traditional interpretation. Many more embraced the promise of a direct relationship with God flowing out of a sincere heart of faith.

Within a decade, the idea that salvation came by "faith alone" had set all of Europe ablaze. Followers of the new "Protestant" movement broke with the ancient Roman Catholic Church, forming a variety of churches under the protection of sympathetic princes and civil authorities. These churches taught followers to reject the Roman Catholic belief that God dispensed his saving grace through the Church, in a set of rituals and observances known as "sacraments." To Protestants, salvation came through faith alone—trust that when Jesus died on the cross, he made full payment for sin and offered forgiveness to those who believed. Many ordinary people across Northern Europe embraced the new ideas for their promise of liberation from burdens of ritual duty and their invitation to a more immediate religious experience. Protestant scholars also translated the Bible into the spoken languages of Europe so that people could read and hear directly what they believed to be the very words of God, unfiltered by layers of Church teaching and tradition.

England had emerged as the champion of Protestant Europe by the time of Anne Marbury's birth in 1591. In the mid-1530s, King Henry VIII and his Parliament broke with Rome through a series of acts and proclamations, made the King the head of the Church of England, and gradually embraced selected Protestant beliefs concerning salvation and the importance of the Bible. Under Henry's son Edward VI (1547–1553), the King's advisors and church officials worked rapidly to eliminate from the Church of England such practices as penance, veneration of the saints, and prayers to Mary. In their view, these rituals were nothing more than idolatry—violations of God's command to worship and pray to none but him. They also attacked idolatry by stripping churches of the statues, ornamentation, and religious art. They regarded these objects as encouraging superstition among the people, tempting them to substitute adoration of mere pictures and carved figures for worship of the true and invisible God. They also instituted new Protestant forms of teaching and practice. They stressed Luther's idea of justification by faith alone. They allowed priests to marry. They placed Bible preaching rather than the ritual of the Mass at the center of English worship.

When Edward died in 1553, however, his Catholic half-sister Mary, the wife of Philip II of Spain, attempted to return England to the Roman Catholic fold. She imprisoned Protestant bishops and clergy, replaced them with faithful Catholic clerics, and restored Catholic forms of worship to the English Church. Marian courts of law eventually condemned many Protestant church leaders to be burned at the stake for heresy, along with many ordinary English Protestant believers. Many others fled to Protestant havens in Continental Europe such as Zurich, Strasbourg, and Geneva, cities where the teachings of the French Reformer John Calvin and his allies were influential. When Mary's brief reign ended with her death in 1558, her half-sister Elizabeth worked to restore England to Protestantism.

Over the next four decades, Elizabeth I worked diligently to secure the Protestant Reformation throughout her realm. She brought back the Protestant exiles from the Continent and made many of them bishops, or leading officers in the English church. She ordered her bishops to compile of a Book of Common Prayer to provide English people with standardized Protestant forms for worship. Besides Protestant prayers and prescriptions for worship, the Elizabethan Prayer Book included a catechism, a brief curriculum of religious instruction based on a statement of core teachings known as the Thirty-Nine Articles. The articles stressed core Protestant beliefs such as justification by faith and the supreme authority of the Bible. They helped to ensure that Protestant ideas would be taught in the English universities where ministers were trained. She commanded every church in her kingdom to provide a copy of the Bible in English. She also required churches to place the Protestant writer John Foxe's *Acts and Monuments,* popularly known as *Foxe's Book of Martyrs,* alongside the Bible. The book collected lurid stories of courageous Protestants who had been imprisoned and died at the stake during Mary's reign, reminding English people of what they had suffered under Catholic rule.

In 1588, just three years before Anne Marbury's birth, English naval forces capped off these internal reforms by scoring a spectacular victory over the massive Spanish Armada. The late Mary Tudor's former husband Philip II of Spain had dispatched this great naval force to conquer England for Catholicism. The English Navy's defeat of this mighty Catholic power established England as the champion of Protestant Europe and a leading contender for Protestant empire in the New World.

Despite these gains, many Protestant leaders believed that the Queen had not taken the Church far enough in the direction of Reformation. Anne's father, Francis Marbury, campaigned against the remaining features of what many termed "popery" in the English church. To win the cooperation of as many English subjects as possible, the "Elizabethan Settlement" of the Church had indeed retained many traditional Catholic forms such as the wearing of priestly garments, making the sign of the cross during baptism, kneeling and rising at prescribed times during worship, and the failure to rid many church buildings of religious ornaments, statuary, and art. In doing so, the Queen and her Parliaments sought to strike a *via media,* or "middle way" of worship, that most English people could live with, if not fully support.

Protestant critics opposed such rituals. They believed that these practices lulled people into a superstitious complacency—a false belief that if they only showed up for services on Sunday, bowed when they were supposed to bow, recited the words of the Prayer Book at the right time, knelt the right way when they received communion, they would make it into heaven. Puritans were convinced that such foolish ideas would send people straight to hell to burn there forever. These critics opposed the ordination of "dumb dogs," ministers who could conduct the services printed in the Prayer Book but were so ignorant they could not even explain what they were reading, much less compose or preach a sermon from the Bible. Such men could not help others find true faith, but could only leave them to die in ignorance of the way of salvation. Many also opposed how the Queen and Parliament retained an "episcopal" form of government for the English church. This hierarchal system centered on bishops, who ruled church affairs within specified districts and appointed ministers or priests to local churches. Bishops had too often shown themselves more interested in grubbing for promotions and lucrative perks rather than the care of souls. Besides this, critics argued, the Bible called for a "presbyterian" system of councils: elders or presbyters appointed by congregations to govern local parishes, and to represent them in regional and national meetings.

English Protestants of Marbury's stripe pursued such reforms to promote greater "godliness" among ordinary Christians and clergy alike. Often labeled "puritan" both by their enemies and, later, historians, these critics followed the teachings of the Reformed branch of Protestantism, often referred to as "Calvinism." Reformed Christianity centered in Switzerland, the German Rhineland, and the Netherlands, and included John Calvin, Ulrich Zwingli, and Heinrich Bullinger among its leading lights. Calvin and other Reformed Protestants embraced Martin Luther's insistence on salvation by faith alone along with his contention that the Bible was the only reliable source of religious knowledge. Yet they went much further than Luther in their rejection of Church tradition. They also emphasized the absolute sovereignty of God over all things and laid special stress on the doctrine of predestination.

By "predestination," Reformed Christians meant that God chose or "elected" certain persons for eternal salvation, without regard for individual human merit. To be sure, a person must believe in order to be saved, but only those chosen by God for salvation would receive the gift of true faith. Reformed theologians debated whether election meant that God merely left the rest of humanity to remain on their natural, unbelieving course to eternal punishment or whether God actively consigned them to hell. Many ministers tempered this harsh verdict by cautioning their parishioners not to despair. After all, one of the thieves crucified with Jesus had repented, believed, and been promised Paradise at the very end of his life. Reformed ministers typically held this belief in predestination in tension with a very active approach to faith and Christian life. Many urged people not to get tied up in knots over questions about whether they were elect or not, but to seize any opportunity to repent and believe. The elect would know themselves elect by believing, and Jesus had promised that he would turn away no one who came to him in true faith. Reformed ministers also followed the language of the Bible by encouraging their followers to pursue active lives of "godly," or devout, conduct in prayer, Bible reading, religious duties, family and community life, and daily affairs.

Historians once saw these beliefs as characteristic of a coherent, well-defined "Puritan" movement which strove for strong Calvinistic theology and eradication of all remaining ritual and ceremony from the English Church, including abolition of bishops and hierarchical church government. Older histories pitted this group against an equally well-defined "Anglicanism" which was thought to have defended a more moderate view of divine grace and human free will, as well as the order and ritualism of the Elizabethan Settlement. Recent research has suggested, however, that a majority of Elizabethan Protestants shared core Reformed beliefs concerning predestination, faith, and godly living despite differences on matters of ceremony and church government. The puritan impulse for reform was fluid in early modern England, varying in both intensity and form across space and time.

As a young Cambridge-educated clergyman, Anne Marbury's father Francis ran afoul of church authorities because of his hot advocacy for puritan-style reform. In 1578 John Aylmer, the Bishop of London, ordered Marbury's arrest and trial for leveling a characteristic presbyterian charge that Elizabeth's bishops were "killing souls" by ordaining ignorant ministers who could not preach. A published transcript of his trial in 1578 before the ecclesiastical, or church-operated, Court of High Commission provides a glimpse of an intelligent, unflappable figure who matched wits with his judges, much as his daughter Anne would do nearly fifty years later in front of the Massachusetts General Court. "Though I fear not you, I fear the Lord," Marbury declared to Bishop Aylmer as he defended his views. Marbury told Aylmer that bishops should ordain only educated ministers who could preach the Bible and Protestant doctrine with power. When one of Aylmer's colleagues exclaimed incredulously, "this fellow would have a preacher in every parish church!" Marbury replied that this was no more than the Bible itself required. Asked by the portly, well-salaried Bishop Aylmer where the money would come from to train such men, Marbury quipped, "A man might cut a good large thong out of *your* hide, and it would not be missed."

Marbury's wit and ability to marshal biblical arguments earned him only Bishop Aylmer's exasperated denunciation as an "overthwart proud puritan knave." Marbury protested that he was "no puritan," but this did nothing to prevent Aylmer from sentencing him to a two-year prison term. There the young minister cooled his heels with other dissidents of the Elizabethan Settlement.

Many of Marbury's fellow convicts probably shared his inability to recognize their discontent with the Church as the puritanism the judges accused them of. In their minds, the only persons deserving such a derogatory tag may have been radical Protestant "Separatists," who viewed the Elizabethan Settlement as too corrupt for reform and the Church of England as no better than the Church of Rome. Separatist Protestants argued that true Christians should simply leave the Church of England and form pure congregations, a strategy the Separatist leader Robert Browne called "Reformation without tarrying for any." This put Separatists on the wrong side of the law and pushed some, such as the group of "Pilgrims" which eventually settled Plymouth Colony, out of England altogether.

Most English Protestants who shared Marbury's convictions saw no need to go so far. They worked from within to reform the Church of England more thoroughly, tolerating whatever ceremonies they thought harmless, and quietly refusing to observe those they regarded superstitious, such as signing the cross at baptism. They did their best to learn the Bible and Protestant doctrine and to order their personal and social lives according to biblical principles. They often referred to one another as "the godly," but the label of puritan has stuck even to those who rejected it during their own lifetime.

After his release from prison in 1580, Francis Marbury settled into a decade of just such a career. He remained in relative conformity with the English church, though evidence suggests that he still maintained ties with the presbyterian movement. He moved to the small market town of Alford in Lincolnshire, where he accepted a post as the town preacher. He also married his first wife, Elizabeth Moore, who bore him three daughters before her death in 1585. Sometime that same year, he accepted a position as schoolmaster of the Alford Free Grammar School. His second marriage in 1586 to Bridget Dryden, daughter of a well-connected puritan family from Northampton, secured his status in the local community, as well as strengthened his links within the English presbyterian network.

Anne was the third child born to Francis and Bridget Marbury, though the fifth in Francis's blended family. The first, Mary, was three years old at the time of Anne's birth, and the second, John, died in infancy the year before. The family also included Elizabeth and Susan, two surviving sisters from the previous marriage. To Protestant families like the Marburys, four girls constituted a "hopeful sign" of God's blessing. "God's favor appeareth in none outward thing more than in increase of children" according to the annotated Geneva Bible, preferred by puritans. If so, the Marburys must have gained an increasing sense of divine approval, as Bridget went on to bear five more girls and seven boys, eight of whom survived to adulthood. The presence of so many younger brothers and sisters gave Anne ample experience in the duties of domestic life. She would grow up to raise a family of similar size.

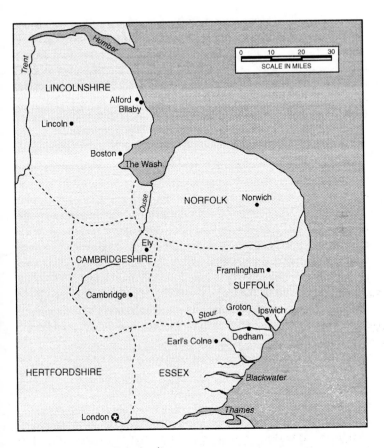

Map 1-1 Greater East Anglia.

The Marburys may have taken Anne's healthy birth as a sign of God's presence in hardship, for in the early 1590s Francis was experiencing a new round of tension with church authorities. The Bishop of Lincoln had ordered him to stop preaching for reasons Francis professed not to know. Yet fresh controversy had recently broken out over the proper form of the English church, and the bishop may have acted against the Marbury family out of suspicion concerning Bridget's connection to puritan family members. The Drydens were among the roughly ten thousand "gentry" families of landowners, some very wealthy and powerful, who together with the hereditary nobility made up the English ruling class. Bridget's influential uncle, Sir Anthony Cope, was part of a block of presbyterian reformers in Parliament where he sat as a member of the House of Commons. In 1587 Cope introduced a bill to replace bishops with a presbyterian organization, in defiance of the Queen's expressed ban on Parliamentary discussion of the issue. To Elizabeth and her councilors, such rash actions posed a threat to her authority which she could ill afford while the King of Spain was assembling a massive force to invade her realm. The Queen's councilors accordingly imprisoned Cope in the Tower of London for his troubles. Bridget's father and elder brother had both developed reputations for protecting puritan ministers from persecution by Elizabeth's bishops. They may also have been involved with clandestine presbyterian synods—governing bodies of ministers eventually intended to replace the bishops. These too posed an unacceptable challenge to royal authority, and the Crown exposed and disbanded them in 1589. The simultaneous publication of a subversive set of anti-episcopal writings known as the "Martin Marprelate" tracts further fanned the flames of controversy.

While Francis Marbury had apparently remained clear of these affairs, he did confess in a letter to authorities of 1590 that he harbored reservations about certain unnamed "points in controversy." This was a polite way of saying that he was not convinced of the official position on issues such as ceremonies and bishops. This was not the most diplomatic admission to make in the superheated atmosphere of the time, especially in the text of a petition to William Cecil, one of the Queen's most trusted councilors. It also did not help that an account of Marbury's clash with the Bishop of London in 1578 was published around this time. His hope for a "dispensation" that would overlook his quibbles with the bishops and restore his pulpit went unanswered until 1594, after the presbyterian agitation had subsided.

Even while temporarily silenced, Francis worked with his wife Bridget to cultivate a puritan family environment for Anne and her siblings. As a "minister of the Word," Francis would have considered it part of his pastoral duty to raise his own family to provide what puritan leaders regarded a model "school for church and commonwealth." Anne's mother would have shared a role in ordering this school of puritan belief and conduct. Anne's sisters and brothers alike would have learned from the household's distinctively Protestant religious education.

Central to the children's education was their need for deliverance from eternal damnation. Calvinist parents such as the Marburys believed that, "through Adam's fall we sinned all," as the *New England Primer*, the famous puritan primary school textbook, would later put it. Like most Christians, they also believed that the sin of humanity's first parents made each person guilty before God and passed to each an irresistible inclination to commit sinful acts. The evidence of this was overwhelming: Good, hard-working, and pious farmers would fly into rages when their neighbor's cattle destroyed their crops. The gentlest and most obedient girls sometimes surrendered to sinful fantasies about the bodies of the young men who were putting a roof on the church. As Anne's contemporary, the poet Anne Bradstreet would put it around 1640:

> Stained from birth with *Adam's* sinfull fact,
>
> Thence I began to sin as soon as act;
>
> A perverse will, a love to what's forbid,
>
> A serpents sting in pleasing face lay hid:
>
> A lying tongue as soon as it could speak,
>
> And fifth Commandment [to honor one's parents] do daily break.

Neither baptism nor good deeds could lift the dreadful curse resulting from "Adam's sinfull fact." The only hope of deliverance from hell, even for a newborn, was that God would choose to grant that person the gift of eternal life through true faith. Divine election was mysterious indeed. Yet God had made a "covenant of grace" with humankind, a formal promise which Jesus sealed with his own sacrificial death. On the cross Jesus suffered the full lethal penalty of human guilt, and he now offered forgiveness and new life to those God elected. God ordinarily reached out to the elect through "the means of grace"— prayer, Bible reading, preaching, the sacraments, and godly conversation—but that person received salvation through God's free gift of faith alone. Anne's parents could at least hope that education would give their children access to these resources and that the children would one day experience true faith and so discover themselves included among the elect.

Anne's mother and father no doubt shared the duty of raising their children "in the instruction and information of the Lord," as the Geneva Bible put it. Very early in the children's lives, they would have begun to teach informally, "speaking to them of good things . . . little and often as they are able to receive." Puritan parents took seriously the Old Testament command to teach their children constantly, "when thou sittest in thine house, and when thou walkest by the waie, and when thou liest downe, and when thou risest up." Anne's parents may well have followed the advice of one writer to teach her the Bible even they were "*dressing* or *undressing*" their daughter "morning and evening."

As Anne and her siblings grew, her parents would have supplemented such casual teaching with regular regimens of instruction and prayer. As father of the house, Francis Marbury bore the duty of formal instruction in the tenets of the Protestant faith. Any English town's schoolmaster and preacher would model a daily routine of religious instruction and psalm singing, supplemented by weekly Sunday evening discussions of that day's sermon. Francis may well have taught Anne the catechism included in the Elizabethan *Book of Common Prayer*, since he insisted that he "subscribed to it and no other for use in the churches." Yet he likely supplemented the rather elementary Elizabethan catechism with large doses of Bible reading and much fuller explanations of key doctrines. As a popular advice manual of the period put it, puritan fathers should teach their children not merely to recite, but to "understand their Catechismes; and be well grounded in all the principles of religion; by a sound and solid knowledge and belief of them, that soe they not forget it."

Anne's mother may have contributed by teaching the children to read the Bible, and certainly would have encouraged her daughter to practice this vital skill. To puritans, the writings of the Old and New Testaments constituted the very Word of God to humankind. As such, it was the primary way of learning about salvation. Puritan readers should take it seriously and as a rule should apply its teachings literally. This belief pushed a growing number of puritan parents to make sure that daughters, as well as sons, could read. To be sure, literacy had already begun to spread among elite English women through the encouragement of humanist scholars of the European Renaissance during the previous two centuries. Even so, Puritans' conviction concerning the importance of reading the Bible set them in the vanguard of efforts to encourage female literacy. Anne became an avid reader of the Bible, with an exceptional capacity to remember, reflect upon, and make use of the things she had read. She also learned how to write, a skill not always taught with reading, and much less common among women than men.

Anne's mother would also have taken charge of preparing the Marbury girls for their "callings." Everyone possessed both a "general calling" to pursue a life of spiritual holiness, or "sanctification," and a "special calling" to the particular life's work which God had prepared for them to do. Unlike her brothers, who could select from a range of vocational options, Anne shared with most other early modern English girls the "special calling" of growing up to become a wife and mother.

Historians have long debated whether the English Reformation created or closed off opportunities for the women of Anne Marbury's day. Some have pointed to Queen Elizabeth's exceptionally long and effective reign as evidence of newfound respect for women's capacities among early modern thinkers and leaders. Others have argued that such Reformation doctrines as the "priesthood of the believer"—the idea that each individual Christian could enjoy equal access to divine favor regardless of sex or ethnicity—laid the foundation for the gradual expansion of opportunities and rights for women in the early modern period.

Yet the most recent historians of early modern women have concluded that, in their beliefs about women, the Reformers did not break sharply with medieval Catholic theologians. Most may have shared with the anonymous Geneva Bible commentator a belief that women were "equal in that which is chiefest (that is to say, in the benefit of eternal life)," but continued to insist that women remained "unequal as touching governance and conversation at home." Reformers shared with their Renaissance and medieval counterparts a suspicion that women were ambitious temptresses by nature, a belief drawn from the Old Testament story of how Eve tempted Adam with forbidden fruit. Reformers noted negative examples such as Delilah, who seduced and brought low the Hebrew judge Samson, and Queen Jezebel, who seduced her husband, King Ahab of Israel, into idolatry and killed the prophets of God. They also cited New Testament passages attributed to St. Paul which commanded women to remain silent in the churches and as subordinates at home.

English Protestants balanced such negative portrayals with positive views of female religious life. Protestant Bible commentators sought to encourage female piety by drawing attention to biblical heroines such as the judge Deborah, who led Israel to victory over their Canaanite foes, and Ruth, the exemplar of Old Testament faithfulness. They noted how Jesus included women among his followers and often pointed to women as positive examples of faith. English pastors took notice when women of their own day followed these biblical precedents, often displaying a spiritual sensitivity greater than that of men. Puritans welcomed women's participation in private meetings, or "conventicles," which gathered for prayer and discussion of the Bible, sermons, doctrine, and Christian living. Some of the women who prayed aloud or spoke during such meetings exhibited an eloquence and spiritual insight greater than most of the men present. This led members of some conventicles to argue that such women ought to take more active roles such as leading in prayer or spiritual discussion, at least within informal gatherings outside of an official church setting. A few radical groups went much further, arguing that no door of religious leadership should be closed to a woman with appropriate gifts and talents.

Nevertheless, the vast majority of Elizabethan Protestants believed that God had restricted women's calling to the domestic sphere, where they should cultivate their spiritual lives as wives and mothers. In this respect they did break decisively with earlier English Catholics, who reserved the term "calling" exclusively for celibate monks and nuns. Historians have also observed that in abolishing the celibate contemplative life, the Reformers actually closed off one of the few alternatives to marriage for women. Indeed, many medieval women had used their status as members of religious orders to carve out significant roles for themselves in Church and society. In breaking with medieval Catholic practice, then, the reformers helped to strengthen English patriarchy—the belief that husbands and fathers should rule in family and society. English law restricted women from buying or selling property, making contracts, or engaging in lawsuits. Any property a woman might inherit became her husband's at marriage. Even her wages belonged legally to her husband.

Reformers did work to temper the harsher effects of patriarchy and encouraged women to take initiative in cultivating rich spiritual lives. They drew on New Testament teachings to promote affectionate marriages and greater mutuality in household and family management. They encouraged wives not merely to pray passively for erring husbands, but to confront them discreetly but firmly. Husbands, in turn, were encouraged to listen to their wives. Reformers discouraged the widespread practice of wife-beating and told wives that they did not have to put up with such treatment. If a husband attempted to force a choice between himself and Christ, the wife should always choose Christ. Puritan women could even turn their subordinate status in home and community to spiritual advantage by stressing how "God resisteth the proud, but giveth grace to the humble." The historian Patricia Crawford has argued that humble pursuit of the religious life enabled puritan English women to develop a distinctive female spirituality, tailored to their own emotional needs and their desire for a sense of communion with the divine. Elizabethan women made religious experience and aspiration very much their own.

Anne Marbury may have begun preparing for her calling as a godly wife and mother as early as five years old, participating in light household tasks such as sweeping, cleaning, and even sewing. At that age, such duties would have punctuated ample periods of "pastime and play." As she grew, her mother would gradually introduce her to the full range of tasks and skills she would need to maintain a household. Along with her elder sisters, she would also assume greater responsibility for supervising the younger Marbury children. Anne's mother probably also introduced her daughter to the art of nursing the sick and midwifery. Such skills were highly valued in an age when doctors were few and medical knowledge sketchy. Proficiency in them would give Anne Marbury an uncommonly prominent role in her family and community.

The year Anne turned fourteen, her father received appointment to the London parish of St. Martin in the Vintry and moved the family there. She was old enough by then for her parents to place her into domestic service, a very common experience for teenage girls in early modern England. Most parents believed their daughters would be more willing to learn manners and industry while living as a productive member of a household other than their own. Anne could have remained in some middling or lesser-gentry household in Alford while the rest of her family lived in London, or she may have gone into service in the city. She may even have split her time between the two locales, since domestics tended to move to new households several times during their years of service. If Anne did go into domestic service, her parents probably sought to place her with a family who shared their religious convictions. They probably also looked for a household where she could continue to develop the skills of nursing the sick, and perhaps begin learning midwifery as deputy to a licensed midwife. She would have continued to hone the manners and bearing needed to become a good wife, mother, and member of the community.

Anne's teenage years were certainly occupied with more than household drudgery. Young women took part in a wide range of pastimes. For puritans, these tended to revolve around religious activities. They condemned many traditional English leisure pursuits such as maypole dances and the frequenting of alehouses. They also frowned upon participation in sport or leisure activities on Sunday, the "Christian Sabbath." Instead, puritan families encouraged their youth to leave no minute wasted in pursuit of their callings. Time spent at work should be complemented with "edifying" pastimes, such as attending sermons or engaging in godly conversation. Weekday lectures supported by wealthy puritan benefactors and delivered by powerful preachers offered one very popular attraction for young people. Puritan ministers also organized periodic fast and thanksgiving days when they would preach an "occasional sermon"—one appropriate to the occasion. They might deliberately choose a date such as May Day to "bear witness against" the day's traditional customs of merry-making and dance.

Like many puritan young people, Anne Marbury probably found such activities stimulating rather than boring. For one thing, she and her puritan friends had spent their childhoods cultivating a taste for sermons and lectures and had learned from their parents and peers how to make a serious game out of criticizing and discussing a minister's ideas and style. Lectures and fasts also provided young people like Anne the opportunity to gather with their friends for extended periods.

Fasts, for example, were usually day-long affairs, including the time spent traveling to the sermon site—often a distance of ten miles or more—and returning home at the end of the day. Mixed groups of male and female "sermon-gadders" set off together early enough in the morning to arrive for a time of socializing with friends and acquaintances from other communities before the formalities opened with a period of prayer. Once the minister began to preach, the travelers settled down to listen for two hours or more. At the end of the sermon, audience members often contributed to a special collection for the poor or "foreign Protestants" who were experiencing persecution or the hardship of war with some Catholic power. This was an act of great idealism for participants, imparting a sense of belonging to a great international movement. At the end of the day's activities, each group might share a meal together before setting out on the return trip home. The time of travel itself provided extended periods for serious conversation as well as lighter socializing.

Any time Anne Marbury went sermon-gadding with other young people to a weekday lecture or fast-day sermon, she would have been welcome to contribute her views to any discussion of the Bible, Christian doctrine, or the day's sermon. In these settings she likely gained familiarity with a wide range of Protestant opinion on points of religious dispute, as well as on issues of the day. She also found a congenial setting for exercising her own considerable intellectual gifts and for honing her ability to express and defend her point of view.

Critics expressed doubt about whether religion was actually the chief topic of interest among young men and women who took day-long trips together across the countryside. Some anti-puritan wits hinted that the journey home after nightfall often afforded lusty young lovers convenient cover to slip away for sexual liaisons. Whatever the grain of truth contained in this slander, sermon-gadding did provide young puritans a common setting for courtship. The teenaged Anne may have often seen her future husband, William Hutchinson, at fast-day sermons or weekday lectures. If living in Alford, she may have gadded along with him to many sermons; if in London, they may have measured their love in miles he traveled to the great city, or to some meeting point in between.

William came from an Alford merchant family who lacked the genteel pedigree of Anne Marbury's extended family. Even so, the evidence suggests that the Hutchinsons were prosperous and capable. The boys probably had some formal education, for William's brothers Samuel and Edward later published books—one in old England, the other in New—which displayed some ability in Latin. This they most likely learned from Anne's father, the local schoolmaster. One or more of the Hutchinson boys may even have shared their schooling with the famous founder of Virginia, John Smith, who also grew up in Alford. As Smith had a knack for military leadership and telling colorful stories, so the Hutchinson boys demonstrated a talent for prospering in the world of trade and exchange. William assumed his father's mercantile enterprise in Alford, a brother John became a draper or maker and seller of woolens and textiles, and another brother Richard a successful ironmonger or dealer in hardware. The Hutchinsons were also well connected with the larger puritan community in Lincolnshire and beyond.

The length of Anne's and William's courtship is unknown. The two probably crossed paths often in Alford during her childhood, but Anne was five years younger than William and may not have captured his heart until sometime after her father moved the family to London in 1605. Anne's father and mother would have taken an active interest in a suitable match that assured good family connections and a comfortable life for their daughter. They would certainly have monitored any associations

Anne struck up with members of the opposite sex, discouraging some and promoting others. The Hutchinson family's prosperity and connections to the puritan community would have made William a very desirable suitor. Under these circumstances, her parents likely followed most of their friends and neighbors in giving Anne space to exercise a modest range of initiative and choice regarding whom she would marry. Sometime during her later teens, the nimble-witted, vivacious young woman won William's respect and devotion.

The death of her father Francis may have given Anne even more freedom of choice than most young women in deciding whom to marry, though almost certainly not in a way she would have wanted. The one-time presbyterian firebrand had served his London parish only six years before dying in 1611. During the last three years of his life he also held two secondary appointments, one at St. Pancras, Middlesex from 1608–1610, and the second, St. Margaret's in London, which he still held at the time of his death. Age must have greatly relaxed Francis Marbury's convictions, for puritans routinely condemned such "plural officeholding." Even so, his dual income probably augmented a family estate substantial enough to provide each surviving child a legacy of nearly £140—a very handsome sum (by way of comparison, John Cotton, distinguished minister of the large and important parish of St. Boltoph's in nearby Boston, received a salary of £100 per year). Francis Marbury's will stipulated that at the age of twenty-one each heir could receive her or his portion and "dwell where they would choose."

Anne Marbury chose to dwell in her old home town as the wife of William Hutchinson. In August, 1612, shortly after Anne's twenty-first birthday, the couple wed at St. Mary Woolnoth in London not far from her father's former parish. Just over nine months later, their first child Edward was baptized in the Alford parish church. Having been brought up puritan, Anne was now launched upon the calling of a devout Protestant Englishwoman.

2

Anne Hutchinson and the Church Militant

Anne Marbury Hutchinson stood defiantly before her judges at the Newton meetinghouse on the second day of her trial in November, 1637, her eyes meeting the astonished stares of the familiar faces surrounding her. John Winthrop, her neighbor and fellow church member, sat directly before her in the governor's seat. Reverend John Cotton, her respected "teacher," stood nearby to testify. Reverend Thomas Shepard, whom she had come to know as her most tenacious accuser, sat with a cluster of ministerial witnesses for the prosecution. Her trial had reached its climactic moment, thanks to her claim that she had received an "immediate revelation" by "the voice of [God's] own spirit to my soul." As she began to elaborate, her thoughts returned to her decision to leave England for America.

"When our teacher [John Cotton] came to New England it was a great trouble to me," Hutchinson recalled. "I was then much troubled concerning the ministry under which I lived." The Spirit of God comforted her with a passage from the Old Testament prophet Isaiah: "Though the Lord give thee bread of adversity and water of affliction yet shall not thy teachers be removed into corners any more, but thine eyes shall see thy teachers." Yet "there was none then left that I was able to hear" within reasonable traveling distance of Alford. With the departure of Cotton and her brother-in-law John Wheelwright, the nearby puritan ministers were gone. "I could not be at rest," she declared, "but I must come hither" to New England.

Hutchinson's speech before the court is studded with enigmatic theological and historical references. Like the tops of tree roots protruding just above the ground, these statements mark the presence of interlacing lines of thought and debate which reach deeply into the previous thirty years of puritan experience in England. Any adequate understanding of her speech and its shocking effect upon her judges must begin with an effort to trace these lines backward into the past and downward into the depths of puritan theological debate and religious experience within an increasingly hostile political environment. Her discontent with the religious scene in her home town of Alford, her sense that all the preachers worth hearing were going into hiding or escaping to New England, her growing conviction that she and her family must follow her teachers to Massachusetts Bay—all stemmed from the impact of great political and religious changes introduced by James I of England and his heir Charles I. The General Court's astonishment at her claim to have heard directly from God stemmed from a tangle of theological debates among puritans. The debates revolved around questions about how a person could know that he or she was saved, how and in what way God might make himself known to a saved person, and what sort of moral obligation a saved person might owe to God and others.

Selected snapshots from the words and deeds of a few important figures in Anne Marbury Hutchinson's life in England and the New World can provide the background needed to make sense of her trial in 1637. Her teacher John Cotton and her brother-in-law John Wheelwright both agonized over how a person could know he or she was elect. A review of their thoughts can begin to illuminate Hutchinson's claim to have heard the very voice of God to her soul. Her critic Thomas Shepard's intense struggle with the same question led him to dabble in ideas swirling around within what some historians have called the "puritan underground" of the early seventeenth century. His experience with these ideas made him deeply uneasy with the views of Cotton, Wheelwright, and Hutchinson, and his unease helps to explain how the controversy in Massachusetts developed as it did. Overarching this ferment of puritan theological discussion and debate was an epic conflict, one pitting puritan defenders of a simplified, purified, Bible-based faith against increasingly aggressive advocates of ceremony, order, form, and hierarchical authority in the English church. By the late 1620s, the puritans' steady loss of ground in this conflict was prompting leaders such as John Winthrop to begin planning a bold new colonial venture in America. A review of this conflict's course can help explain why families like the Hutchinsons were considered prime candidates for the colony, and why Anne and William eventually joined thousands of others in sailing for Massachusetts Bay.

Anne Marbury Hutchinson came of age, married, and began her family during one of the most turbulent periods in England's history. 1603 saw not only a new ruler but a new dynasty when James Stuart, James VI of Scotland, succeeded Elizabeth Tudor as James I of England. The puritans of England held high hopes for this reputed Calvinist king of staunchly Presbyterian Scotland. They expected him to favor their plan to complete the reformation of the Church of England, which in their view had stalled under Elizabeth I. They also hoped for aggressive support of Protestantism throughout the European world, and financing to establish a series of Protestant New World colonies, to counter Spain's Catholic empire there. With its fabled wealth in gold and silver and its vast potential for trade, the New World held high hopes for wealthy families.

The boosters of New World Empire saw their hopes turn into reality; the supporters of Reformation did not. During the next twenty years, puritan leaders found themselves increasingly on the defensive by the ecclesiastical policies—those concerning the forms and government of the Church of England—followed by the new Stuart rulers, King James and his son, Charles I. The networks established during Elizabeth's reign continued, supporting puritan preachers and encouraging puritan laypeople, even as they were driven further underground. During this period, the theological beliefs of various puritan leaders continued to evolve and shift on matters such as the proper organization of the church and the relationship of saving grace to good works. This produced greater diversity among those who thought of themselves as "godly Protestants." Surviving records provide only fleeting glimpses of the Hutchinsons during these years, but the changes swirling around them exerted a profound impact.

After ascending the throne, James I acted quickly to address the pent-up religious grievances of his new English subjects, though not in the way "hotter sorts of Protestant" such as the Hutchinsons had hoped. They anticipated a sympathetic hearing from a king who professed Calvinist views and came from a Presbyterian land. So high were their expectations that a distinguished group of reformers rushed to meet James as he arrived from Scotland to begin his reign, bringing with them a petition reputedly signed by a thousand ministers. The Millenary Petition, which took its name from the number of signers, called for modest reforms in church government and the elimination of certain rituals deemed "popish," such as liturgical music, bowing at the name of Jesus, and making the sign of the cross in baptism.

In January 1604, James I chaired the Hampton Court Conference, which he had convened in response to the Millenary Petition. There he listened to grievances. He also took the opportunity to display his own great learning by participating actively in the theological debate among England's leading clergy. The king promised some minor reforms, including a more accurate and updated translation of the Bible now known as the "King James Version." However, his staunch defense of the existing hierarchy of bishops and prayer book ceremonies disappointed the reformers. In the months after the conference his newly appointed archbishop, Richard Bancroft, published a new Book of Canons, a set of ecclesiastical regulations upholding traditional church government and its rituals. All clergy had to sign or swear to support these canons. Between seventy and eighty salaried puritan ministers conscientiously refused and were dismissed. Over two hundred more who ministered voluntarily in various capacities were disqualified from preaching, teaching, or serving in the Church. Far more settled into an uncomfortable conformity with the new requirements. Most abandoned further reform efforts and worked to cultivate within the Church an atmosphere of toleration for the occasional acts of nonconformity produced by a tender puritan conscience.

The king's decision at Hampton Court frustrated not only puritans but English Catholics too, so much so that it confirmed a small group of Catholic conspirators in their attempt to assassinate James I and blow his Parliament to bits. Its members hatched the notorious Gunpowder Plot in the hope that the destruction of the Protestant king and his Parliament would clear the way for England's return to the Catholic fold. The plot backfired when, late on the night of November 4, 1604, agents of James I discovered conspirator Guy Fawkes in a basement room packed with thirty-six barrels of gunpowder. Just hours later, the king, crown prince, and Parliament would meet in the chamber above. Fawkes was waiting for that moment to ignite a blast that would blow them all sky high. The discovery confirmed most English people in their worst fears of Catholic treachery and rallied them to the king and Protestantism. It also made November 5—the day that James and his Parliament survived—a holiday which is still celebrated in England.

Nevertheless, the king steadfastly maintained the ecclesiastical status quo, prompting the majority of puritan ministers and laypeople to shift tactics. Blocked in their efforts for further reform, they sought to defend whatever toeholds they had gained and to win toleration of their views wherever possible. Wealthy patrons continued to support existing puritan lectureships and to establish new ones. Puritan ministers continued to insist that preaching and active pastoral care, not formal observance of ceremonies, remained the most important parts of their job. In many places, an influential puritan family would extend protection to a local minister, helping to screen his activities from the bishop's attention or appealing to the bishop's sympathy for puritan ideas if possible. When nothing else worked, puritan leaders sometimes swallowed their scruples against corruption in the Church and bribed officials to look the other way.

In these ways, many puritan clergy and laypeople gained space to strip away the showy forms that could so easily mask hypocrisy or meaningless performance and pursue a heartfelt, sincere, faith based on the Bible. If possible, puritan ministers left their priestly robes on a hook in a corner and conducted services in plain clothes. They omitted or shortened rote recitation from the prayer book and left out as much of the kneeling, bowing, and cross-signing as they could get by with. They pointed out that the Book of Common Prayer itself termed such practices *adiaphora*, or "matters indifferent," and they argued that any attempt to enforce these ceremonies violated the prayer book by transforming them into requirements. Puritan laypeople relished good preaching wherever they could find it, even if that meant skipping dull services in their own parish church to catch a good sermon in a neighboring one.

This was the kind of ministry Anne Hutchinson apparently longed for but could not find at the Alford parish church during her years there. She was most likely "much troubled" for the same reasons as other puritan laypeople: her vicar followed the prescribed forms of the Book of Common Prayer. He wore the priestly garments, read the prayers, and performed the rituals. Such rote observance could not satisfy Hutchinson's deep longing for an experience of spiritual union with God, nor could it answer her agonizing questions or those of her neighbors and friends. How could she know she was one of God's elect? How could she be sure her faith was real—that she was not simply deceiving herself? What spiritual help could she offer her child troubled by recurrent nightmares of torment in hell? How could she help the family of the devout young mother who had suffered so cruelly and died in childbirth? The Alford vicar's canned prayers and empty ceremonies held no answers.

The town of Boston fifteen miles away, however, had a minister with a growing reputation for personal godliness and powerful preaching. John Cotton became vicar of St. Botolph's Church there at about the time the newlywed Anne and William Hutchinson moved to Alford. Puritan-leaning officials of Boston were eager to offer the post to one of the best preachers to graduate from Emmanuel College, Cambridge, which was the foremost center of puritan learning in England. The bishop of the diocese of Lincoln, where Boston was located, objected at first to the appointment. He deemed Cotton too young a man to be appointed to the pulpit of a town with a reputation for vigorous nonconformity, or resistance to the forms of worship prescribed in the Book of Common Prayer. The town leaders knew how to make the objection go away: they placed a bribe with one of the bishop's influential aids. Cotton was installed without further incident.

John Cotton had to swear to support the bishops and observe the prescribed ceremonies "as containing nothing contrary to the Word of God" just as Hutchinson's vicar at Alford had done. Yet Cotton soon made clear that Bible preaching, not prayer book rites, formed the heart and soul of his ministry. He soon added a Thursday lecture to his Sunday ministry. Before long he also began avoiding many ceremonies which conflicted with his conscience, and his bishop even suspended him briefly for nonconformity because of this. Eventually, the town hired a second "mayor's chaplain" to perform the ceremonies. Cotton, meanwhile, produced a "feast of preaching" at St. Botolph's that drew people from the surrounding countryside to hear him. Anne Hutchinson may have traveled from Alford a number of times, perhaps bringing her growing family in tow, to attend his sermons and lectures.

Cotton shared with other Calvinist ministers a belief that God had predestined some people to eternal life and framed this theological commitment into a message filled with hope for listeners such as the Hutchinsons. Through the "covenant of grace," God's unconditional promise of salvation, the elect among them—those chosen for salvation—could know without a doubt that their faith was sincere and not a sham. They could be confident that they had received God's gracious gift of salvation and could enjoy a life of spiritual intimacy with God. Puritan ministers called this knowledge "assurance" and saw it as a work of God's Holy Spirit. The Spirit did not want an elect, believing child to wake up with night terrors of hellfire. God wanted to comfort that child, providing reassurance that he or she was saved.

Cotton's preaching followed the common Calvinist account of how a believer could receive this assurance of their elect status. He stressed how to prepare for salvation through a process of prayerful introspection, reading of Scripture, and listening to edifying sermons. A young man must recognize that his angry outbursts were symptoms of a much deeper problem, a heart that was rotten to the core. He might try to make amends for his hurtful words or flying fists, might try to balance the harm done in one situation by a good deed somewhere else, but he could never do enough to rescue himself from the fires of hell. His duplicitous heart could be endlessly inventive, masking resentment or self-pity behind a superficial sense of sorrow for injuring a friend, or covering self-righteous complacency with an outward show of piety. Like an alcoholic addicted to liquor, an angry young sinner could not break free of sin on his own. He was perpetually in denial. He was totally unable to repent or save himself. He needed the help of a higher power. Only God's Spirit could open the eyes of his heart to see truly and grieve sincerely his utter spiritual bankruptcy. Only the Spirit could enable him to embrace Jesus through the gift of true faith. Only that faith could assure him that he had truly received forgiveness.

Puritans knew this moment of spiritual insight and faith as "conversion." True converts might in that moment also receive an "immediate witness of the Spirit" who assured them of salvation by taking some promise of Scripture—often a familiar passage such as Ephesians 2:8, "For by grace you are saved through faith"—and transforming it into an intimate personal message of "ravishing joy," as if spoken directly to the believing reader's soul. Anne Hutchinson described her own experience of conversion, true faith, and assurance in terms very much like these.

Many puritan ministers accepted the idea that elect individuals could receive assurance through the witness of the Spirit, but cautioned that this was neither the only means of assurance nor always the most reliable. Believers must also monitor their "sanctification"—their devotion to God and their practice of good works in daily life—for signs of grace. A woman who thought she had believed and received assurance, but who neglected to pray and read her Bible regularly, or who cultivated a sinful taste for vicious gossip as if it were an innocent pastime, might well be deceiving herself. She might be making the fatal assumption that she could simply presume upon God's readiness to forgive. Yet she could also err in the other direction. She could speak only good of her neighbors, help a friend with a sick child, never miss a sermon—and do it all for the wrong reason. She might be laboring "under a covenant of works," harboring in her heart the idea that God would only save her if she did these good deeds. True sanctification lay along a fine line between complacency and "works righteousness." But those whose deeds and attitudes flowed from sincere and increasing faith could base their sense of assurance on the evidence of a godly life, even if they never received a direct inner witness of the Spirit.

John Cotton eventually broke from this widespread view of assurance—one we will call "sanctificationist"—to stress the importance of the Spirit's witness in a way that would later prompt Anne Hutchinson to see him as a kindred spirit. Remembering back on his ministry at St. Botolph's from a much later time, Cotton recalled that at some point he began to tell his parishioners there that true assurance could come only by an inward, personal encounter with the Spirit of God "before works." Assurance never "followed after." In comparison to such a soul-ravishing experience, a believer's holy attitudes and behavior offered "no more evidence" of assurance "than a Candle in the Sun." At best, a search for assurance in good works could reveal no more than the person already known by true faith.

If Cotton did begin preaching this way while at St. Botolph's, he was taking sides in a debate over assurance in which other ministers were prepared to go even further. Anne Hutchinson's brother-in-law, John Wheelwright, was ready to suspect many sanctificationists of weakening the covenant of grace and opening the door to "works righteousness." Wheelwright and others worried that such thinking would obscure the Reformation doctrines of "grace alone" and "faith alone." Divine grace was free, they insisted. God could dispense it as he wished with no conditions attached. No good work could be offered in payment for grace. Champions of this idea of "free grace" warned that the practice of looking to sanctification for evidence of grace slipped all too easily into a habit of reliance on good works for salvation.

Anne Hutchinson eventually came to side with her brother-in-law and John Cotton on a free-grace belief that assurance came only through the inner witness of God's Spirit. It is uncertain whether she adopted her free-grace views from Cotton, her brother-in-law, some circle of puritan friends, or even her own reading of the Bible, but she certainly dated her initial experience of the Spirit's inner witness during her time in Alford. Hutchinson eventually came to maintain that, in Cotton's teaching, she could detect the Spirit of Jesus (she called this "the voice of my beloved") bearing inward witness with her spirit to the covenant of grace.

Hutchinson's notion of an inward divine voice carried with it some very potent dangers, however. How could she tell that the voice was really God's? What if the voice told her to do something crazy like taking off all her clothes in front of her neighbors or breaking her marriage covenant to sleep with another man? What if it told her she was the Messiah and charged her to lead a bloody revolution against the King? Rumors abounded in early modern England of people who did just these kinds of things because an inner voice told them to. If God had spoken in the Bible, wasn't that enough? After all, another key Reformation doctrine was *sola scriptura,* the "Bible alone." What sorts of control on belief remained if people began listening to inward voices along with the Bible, or instead of it?

These were exactly the kinds of questions that troubled Thomas Shepard and eventually made him one of Anne Hutchinson's most determined adversaries when he encountered her ideas in New England. His concerns arose out of his own experience in the 1620s as an undergraduate at John Cotton's alma mater, Emmanuel College, Cambridge. There Shepard's journey toward conversion and faith began as he listened to the preaching of the college master and royal chaplain John Preston. Preston's words plunged the young man into a period of excruciating self-examination for evidence that God had chosen him for salvation. Shepard's quest for true faith and assurance temporarily led him to the popular minister Roger Brereley, who preached at a chapel in Grindleton in the northern county of Yorkshire. Brereley was known for "a mighty possessing, over-powering presence and work of the spirit." He enjoyed some support among the clergy and participated in the larger puritan ministerial network.

Beyond the preaching, what attracted Shepard and many other puritans to Grindleton was Brereley's contention that the efforts of preparation which many other puritans had encouraged were utterly useless. He taught that true faith could come to a bright young person like Thomas Shepard only if he became humble enough to "sit in . . . ignorance" and wait "in the word of Truth, till the light shines." No amount of university learning or private introspection could conjure up this moment of spiritual enlightenment. But when it came, Brereley taught, Christ would be spiritually "born to" a believer like Shepard, taking up residence in his life in a way analogous to the Virgin Mary carrying the unborn Jesus in her womb. This spiritual invasion and union with Jesus could give the young Shepard "the mind of

Christ," a new set of dispositions and ways of thinking which enabled him to imitate Jesus himself. Finally, conversion would release Shepard from the onerous burdens of the Law of God, freeing him to serve Jesus out of true love for God and others.

To Shepard's puritan teachers at Emmanuel, Brereley's ideas smacked of dangerous "antinomianism." Derived from the Greek prefix "anti" (against) coupled with "nomos" (law), the term literally meant "against the law." Theologians of the day applied the label to a spectrum of beliefs which suggested that in some way or other, Jesus' death had superseded God's moral code expressed in the Ten Commandments, draining God's law of any force for Christians. If this were true, critics warned, good works did not matter. Not only did a person not need to prepare for grace; a true believer with the "mind of Christ" did not have to worry about God's law. True faith freed them from the law. They could do as they pleased.

Roger Brereley did indeed teach something like this notion that true believers were liberated from bondage to divine law. Thomas Shepard flirted with this idea and Anne Hutchinson may eventually have come to believe it. In fairness, however, Brereley and others like him thought that this was so because the "mind of Christ" within a believer made that person both unshakably certain of his salvation and morally perfect, no longer able to desire or "committ a gross sinne." Yet to mainstream puritans, this very notion could invite gross hypocrisy by denying the self-evident struggle with sin that continued to plague any Christian who was truly honest with himself or herself. At worst, it could lead to the idea that nothing a Christian did was sin, opening the door to total moral chaos.

Indeed, behind these fears of antinomianism—fears which mainstream puritans shared with the staunchest supporters of the English prayer book—lay two specters of total social and moral chaos. The first was an antinomian revolt which took place in the German city of Muenster nearly a hundred years before. In 1534 a group of radical reformers took control of the prosperous city. Before long, the leadership of this revolt passed to a charismatic young tailor known as John of Leiden, who proclaimed himself a new messiah charged with ushering in God's thousand-year reign on earth. John's followers seized property and redistributed it among the inhabitants of Muenster. They systematically destroyed all the city's religious art and sculpture. They killed all opponents. They instituted polygamy. Some even argued for abolishing marriage altogether. Appalled Protestant rulers joined forces with Catholic authorities to recapture the city, execute John of Leiden, and restore order, but not before Muenster had become a symbol of the moral and civil chaos associated with radical religious ideas.

The second specter that haunted puritan fears was a movement called the "Family of Love." Its sixteenth-century Dutch founder, Hendrik Niclaes, believed that "personal revelations" delivered by God superseded the Bible. The chosen few who received such divine messages entered a mystical union with Christ. This union freed them from sin, and the obligation to observe the law of God. "Familists" were suspected of using this idea of sinless perfection to ignore the bond of marriage and morality and to enjoy sexual promiscuity between male and female sect members, a practice termed "the community of women." This may be what Thomas Shepard had in mind when he later recalled Niclaes's assertion that a believer under the Spirit's influence could commit "even whoredom, and it is no sin."

Familist influence had almost died out by Shepard's and Anne Hutchinson's day. Preachers such as Roger Brereley vigorously denied any link between Niclaes's ideas and theirs. Nevertheless, the fear of antinomian moral chaos drove Shepard back to a rigorous sanctificationist program of self-examination and holy living for evidence that his faith was genuine and he truly elect. The knowledge he had gained from his brush with reputed antinomians made him one of many expert heresy hunters among the puritan clergy. Shepard eventually brought to New England a skill for listening critically to the details of his congregation's ideas about God and the Christian life.

Thomas Shepard knew that puritan laypeople thought for themselves—the very character of their faith demanded it. A growing percentage of puritan farmers and tradesmen learned to read the Bible at Sunday sermons and lectures, often disagreeing with their ministers over the meaning of a passage. Puritan women—such as Anne Hutchinson read the Bible in private devotion, purchased pamphlets about the Christian life, discussed theological issues in the home, and formed their own opinions from their reading and discussion. Shepard worried that even an innocent misreading of scripture could divert a parishioner into error—even into the fires of hell. Smart, articulate, literate laypeople like Hutchinson might not only think their way into error, but become agents of error themselves. Their beliefs needed constant monitoring to avert such disaster.

Shepard's finely honed ability to detect heresy would eventually bring him into conflict with Anne Hutchinson in New England, but in the 1620s the two would quite likely have considered themselves on the same side of a great conflict with a new breed of English bishop. During this decade, a longstanding Calvinist consensus within the Church of England began to break down. In previous years, puritan ministers had often clashed sharply with bishops over the government and ceremonies of the Church even as the two sides shared allegiance to the Calvinist teachings expressed in the Church's Thirty-Nine Articles of Religion. James I supported this Calvinist consensus through much of his reign. In 1618 he even sent committed Calvinist bishops to represent the Church of England at the Synod of Dordt in the Netherlands, which met to condemn the anti-Calvinist teachings of the Dutch theologian James Arminius.

Yet shortly thereafter he began appointing bishops from a group of anti-Calvinist clergy the puritans labeled "Armenian." Led by Richard Neile, the Bishop of Durham, this growing cluster of like-minded associates came to be known as the Durham House Group. Its members shared a zealous embrace of episcopacy, a sharp antipathy to the doctrine of predestination, and a deep conviction that divine grace was available to all through the ceremonies and sacraments of the Church of England. In 1621 James appointed one of Neile's protégés, William Laud, to the small bishopric of St. David's and made him a member of the royal court. There Laud's star rose rapidly, drawing other anti-Calvinist clergy in its train. He became a favorite of the king's closest advisor, George Villiers, the first Duke of Buckingham. When the throne passed to Charles I upon James's death, the new king had Laud appointed as Bishop of London in 1627 and installed as Archbishop of Canterbury in 1633, all the while entrusting him with ever greater control of Church affairs.

Laud implemented a rigorous program of ecclesiastical reform. His plan included potent symbolic changes in the arrangement of church furnishings, strict enforcement of Prayer Book ceremonies, and efforts to beautify worship through music and ritual. He required that all ministers wear vestments—ornamental robes—when conducting services, that they make the sign of the cross in baptism, that they bow at the name of Jesus, and that they encourage parishioners to do the same. He taught that the cups and plates used in the rite of the Lord's Supper were holy because they contained Jesus' special presence in the bread and wine. They were to be touched with utmost reverence by the priest alone, as was the communion table that held them. Laud placed church communion tables "altar-wise," or parallel, to the east wall of churches and chapels as in Roman Catholic churches and fenced them off to restrict access only to the clergy. He took vigorous action against any minister who refused to conform to the required church ceremonies, and worked to curtail Calvinist preaching throughout the realm.

These were likely the kinds of changes which troubled Anne Hutchinson so much at her home parish in Alford. Every Sunday the new arrangements—the orientation of the communion tables, the decorous behavior of the robed vicar, the rote prayers, the tedious cycle of standing, bowing, and kneeling—confronted puritans with immediate, compelling evidence that Laud and his bishops were trying to dismantle the Protestant Reformation. Hutchinson and others who sympathized with her may have mounted some protest, but laypeople were finding it increasingly risky to do so. Refusal to conform to the prayer book ceremonies—by standing, for example, when everyone else knelt—could earn the offender a reprimand or a fine.

Puritan ministers faced much higher stakes, for refusal to conform placed their very livelihoods in jeopardy. Hutchinson and other puritan laypeople could only watch helplessly as Laud and his bishops began summoning nonconforming clergy before the Court of High Commission, a special court established by the Crown to enforce the laws and regulations of the English Church. The bishops frequently used this court to silence such men, forbidding them to preach or speak publicly beyond mere recitation of the words of official ceremony. They dismissed many others from their positions. In 1630, Laud himself ordered Thomas Shepard not to teach in London, remarking, "I will have no such fellows prate in my diocese." When John Cotton learned of his summons to appear before the High Court in 1632, he took refuge in a clandestine network of puritan clergy and their supporters. Many other ministers joined Shepard and Cotton in the early 1630s, surfacing briefly to preach, then slipping back under cover to evade capture by Laudian authorities.

Anne Hutchinson's sense of trouble under her own parish ministry suggests that she, like other puritans, viewed the Laudian program as a shocking return to hated Roman Catholic practice. Laud's changes in the treatment of communion tables became the most potent symbol of their fears. Not only did his bishops fence the tables and move them altar-wise; they actually restored many of the stone altars which sixteenth century Reformers had shattered. Laud placed Communion rather than preaching at the center of English worship. To treat the simple ritual of the Lord's Supper with such pomp and ceremony strongly suggested that Laud was secretly working to restore the Roman Catholic doctrine of transubstantiation—in which the bread and wine of Communion literally transformed into Christ's body and blood—and with it to the whole system of Catholic belief and practice. Puritans suspected a nefarious plot—emanating perhaps from the influence Henrietta Maria, the French Catholic wife of Charles I—to make England Catholic once again. This prospect prompted Anne Hutchinson to join many puritans in contemplating a drastic step her father would never have considered—total separation from the Church of England to form a pure Protestant church, one free of "popish ceremony."

The temptation to separate only intensified when puritans contemplated the implications of Charles's marriage to a French Catholic. To Hutchinson and many others, the realm appeared to be shifting decisively to the wrong side of what they saw as a cosmic struggle between the Protestant forces of the true faith and a Roman Catholic counterfeit. Puritans saw the pope as none other than the Antichrist of the Apocalypse, who usurped the crown of King Jesus with his own claim to be the "Vicar of Christ." The Catholic rulers of Europe were his lackeys, and Satan himself orchestrated the whole from his throne of darkness. As puritans saw it, James I had first dallied with these forces of evil by trying to marry Charles off to a Spanish princess. Having failed in that, he had subsequently succeeded with France. Furthermore, he refused to help his own Calvinist son-in-law Frederick V, ruler of the German-speaking Palatine region along the Rhine River, whose armies were taking a beating from Catholic forces in a conflict known to history as the Thirty Years War.

In fact, the Thirty Years War confronted both James and Charles after him with an extremely complicated series of diplomatic, fiscal, and military challenges. Both did their best to promote English diplomatic, religious, and fiscal interests—the last of these being a very good reason for staying out of the conflict. Yet to puritans steeped in the imagery of biblical prophecy and convinced that the Pope was the very arch-enemy of Jesus, this could only mean that God's patience was wearing thin. England was teetering on the brink of divine judgment. Anne Hutchinson later expressed a common puritan viewpoint on the matter, when at her arrival in Massachusetts she declared her expectation that "England should be destroyed."

This sense of impending doom prompted many puritans to begin considering a bold new step: flight from the doomed realm of England to establish a new puritan refuge in America. In 1628 a small group of veteran promoters of New World colonization worked with new puritan investors to form a new joint-stock enterprise, the New England Company, to establish a colony in Massachusetts Bay. Although Anne Hutchinson later hinted that she was not among the first to think of leaving England, she certainly watched with interest as the plans became reality.

The New England Company obtained a patent for their colony March 4, 1629. Organizers wasted no time in recruiting new investors and potential colonists for the "Governor and Company of the Massachusetts Bay in New England," as the royal patent renamed the company. John Winthrop, though an obscure Suffolk gentleman, was the kind of man the company was looking for, a person of "worth and quality," willing to move his family to New England and share in the "government of the plantation." Winthrop's family had supported puritan causes for three generations from its seat at Groton manor. Winthrop himself had undergone a conversion experience in his youth, and had dedicated himself to a life of disciplined holy living. He had supported puritan interests through his training in law and through his influence as an officeholder both in his home county and in London. He now saw a new avenue for the use of his resources and talents in Massachusetts Bay. Throughout the spring and summer of 1629, he corresponded with family and friends while meeting with other interested colonists, including John Cotton and two other ministers who would soon make a name in the New World—Thomas Hooker, a founder of Connecticut, and Roger Williams, the founder of Rhode Island. The distinctive purpose of the new colony to establish an outpost of puritan English society in America began to crystallize through these conversations and Winthrop's own internal debate about whether a man of his age and station should "adventure his whole family" upon such an uncertain enterprise.

By August 1629, Winthrop had decided to go. On the twenty-sixth he met with twelve other leaders at Cambridge University to sign a joint pledging "without scruple" to "dispose of his estate and affairs," and to "be ready in our persons, and with such of our several families as are to go with us . . . by the first of March next." Winthrop began a flurry of preparations to fulfill his part of the pledge and to recruit additional colonists for the voyage. Two days later, a meeting of company directors known as the "General Court" voted to transfer the entire government of the company, including its charter, to Massachusetts. This unprecedented move would make the colony virtually self-governing, putting three thousand miles of ocean between the company directors and any interference by the Crown, the bishops, or powerful rivals. Winthrop began meeting with the General Court in September. At a mid-October meeting the body elected him Governor to replace the outgoing Matthew Craddock. It also elected three councilors, Richard Saltonstall, Isaac Johnson, and John Humfry, to round out a "Court of Assistants."

Under Winthrop and his associates, Massachusetts Bay took on a set of principles distinctive from those of other English colonial enterprises. In addition to the standard reasons for colonization, such as increased seafaring trade, employment for the English population, and expansion of England's claim to empire, settlers in Winthrop's Massachusetts would serve a distinctly puritan mission. Colonists would build a "bulwark against the kingdom of Antichrist which the Jesuits labor to raise in all parts of the world." They would find a refuge from divine judgment on England. They would establish a new center of puritan learning, free from the "evil examples and licentious government" so destructive of youthful morality in the English universities. They would "help raise and support a particular church . . . in the bud and infancy of its life." Colonists would be drawn primarily from those "known to be godly" who would set an example of sacrifice by forsaking their "wealth and prosperity" to "run the hazard . . . of a hard and mean condition."

Most significantly for its long-term stability and success, recruits for Massachusetts Bay Colony made a decision about its composition which would make Anne and William Hutchinson ideal candidates for recruitment. Most colonial schemes of the time focused on recruiting able-bodied young men to work as artisans and indentured servants. The founders of Massachusetts, however, would recruit independent heads of households and their families. This decision would avert the chronic instability and population drain which had afflicted Virginia and troubled English ventures in the Caribbean as well. To be sure, Massachusetts Bay colonists would supplement their labor needs with servants and company employees: servants constituted twenty-five percent of those migrating to New England in the 1630s. Even so, the decision to focus primarily on families would bless New England with a gender-balanced, self-sustaining residential and agricultural society.

During the fall and winter of 1629–1630, Winthrop worked from London to direct an intensive recruiting effort, reaching deeply into the puritan networks through his own extensive ties of family, friends, and associates. These agents circulated manuscript copies of "General Observations," written largely by Winthrop, which listed reasons for migration to New England. They also circulated Reverend Francis Higginson's *New England's Plantation*, a glowing first-hand account which promised prospective colonists that the very air of New England was "better than a whole draught of old England's ale." Puritan clergy read both documents from their pulpits. Puritan gentry held meetings in their homes to recruit colonists. Ministers and gentlemen forwarded names and recommendations for interested colonists to Winthrop and other company officials in London.

By the target date of March 1, 1630, Winthrop and his associates had recruited enough colonists to fill eleven ships. Throughout the month, the governor made final preparations, welcomed the families departing for New England, and oversaw the lading of vessels waiting in the harbor at Southampton. A few days prior to sailing, John Cotton preached the colonists a farewell sermon. He tellingly compared their venture to the Protestant exiles of Mary Tudor's day, who fled England after Mary proclaimed her realm Catholic. Winthrop himself may also have preached his sermon, *A Model of Christian Charity,* at this time. In it, he reminded colonists that they had made a covenant with God to "improve our lives to do more service to the Lord," to strengthen the church and its members, and to preserve themselves and their descendants "from the common corruptions of this evil world." If they kept the covenant faithfully, Winthrop predicted that its resulting success would prompt founders of subsequent colonies to hope the Lord would "make it like that of New England." Massachusetts was in fact "a city on a hill" with "the eyes of all people upon us." On March 29, Winthrop boarded the company flagship, the *Arbella,* and set sail with three other ships. The other seven followed a month later.

This began the Great Migration to New England. During the next decade, more than 21,000 men, women, and children would leave their homes in England to create a new society an ocean away. Historians have long debated the reasons why so many decided to sell everything and move their families across the Atlantic. Few have questioned the motivational ability of religious leaders such as Winthrop, but some historians have pointed out that an economic depression in early seventeenth-century England may also have influenced ordinary colonists. A downturn in the textile market was squeezing the weavers, spinners, and merchants who formed East Anglia's economic base. Even Winthrop struggled to meet expenses, and his "General Observations" noted how difficult it had become "for a good and upright man to maintain his charge and to live comfortably in his profession." John Cotton declared in his farewell sermon that God permitted migration when the "Common-wealth is so full, that Tradesmen cannot live one by another, but eat up one another." Such considerations undoubtedly prompted some to

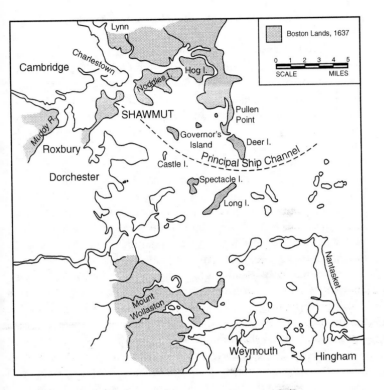

Map 2-1 Boston Harbor.

migrate so they could maintain their own status in life and secure an inheritance for their children. Indeed, many of the 5,000 who came as servants may have done so for exclusively economic reasons. Yet most historians now agree that such concerns need not have precluded religious motivations. Most families likely took both into account.

The Hutchinson family certainly fit this pattern of mixed economic and religious motives for migration. Whatever religious reasons William and Anne Hutchinson may have shared for leaving England, they also needed a reliable source of livelihood to feed, clothe, and house a family, especially one which had grown to eleven children when they embarked for Massachusetts Bay in 1634. As a well-to-do cloth merchant, William possessed the capital to set up a transatlantic textile trade when he arrived in Massachusetts Bay. When he sold his family estate in Alford, he very likely followed the common practice of investing the proceeds in a stock of cloth for New England. He could sell the cloth for profit or exchange it for the agricultural goods and services the family needed to establish itself in the Bay Colony.

William Hutchinson also brought an extensive transatlantic network of business contacts with him composed largely of family members and friends. Some came with him to New England; others remained at home. Within two years of his arrival in Boston, William entered a joint venture with fourteen other partners to build a dock, wharf, and crane in Boston harbor. There the partners could load and offload the cargo of transatlantic merchant vessels. Viewed from this perspective, the move to Massachusetts opened an attractive opportunity for William Hutchinson and his associates to expand their business. Indeed, the extended Hutchinson family survived the turmoil of the 1630s to become a fixture in the colonial mercantile community.

Even considering the economic factors, Anne Hutchinson's testimony at her trial in 1637 demonstrates that religious motivations dominated the family's decision to move. As for many other migrants, her restlessness originated in discontent with "the falseness of the constitution of the Church of England," an aversion so strong that she "had like to have turned separatist." This discontent likely coincided with the intensified anti-Calvinist campaign which drove John Cotton underground in 1632 and caused Hutchinson's "brother Wheelwright" to lose his parish shortly after.

With Cotton on his way to New England, and Wheelwright no longer preaching, Hutchinson found comfort only after the Spirit "brought to her mind" Isaiah 30:20, "though the Lord give thee bread of adversity and water of affliction yet shall not thy teachers be removed into corners any more, but thine eyes shall see thy teachers." Since Hutchinson no longer expected her eyes to see Cotton in England, she concluded that the Spirit was calling her and her family to "come hither" to Massachusetts Bay. William, who respected his wife as a "dear saint and servant of God," agreed. In late June 1634, the Hutchinson family boarded the *Griffin* to follow Hutchinson's revered teacher to New England.

3

A Profitable Member among Us

"Mrs. Hutchinson, you are called here as one of those that have troubled the peace of the commonwealth and the churches here," John Winthrop declared. The newly reelected governor of Massachusetts Bay Colony opened the trial with a list of her offenses. She had contributed "a great share" in promoting the opinions which had set Massachusetts boiling with controversy over the past two years. She was closely associated with other dissenters whom the Court had already punished for their own roles in the trouble. She had said things "very prejudicial to the honor of the churches and ministers." She had kept a meeting in her house which the General Court had condemned as "not tolerable nor comely in the sight of God nor fitting for your sex." "We have thought good to send for you," the governor explained, to persuade her to renounce her errors, "so that you may become a profitable member here among us." If this effort failed, the court would banish her so that "you may trouble us no further."

To submit to the General Court's will and become a "profitable" community member on the one hand, or to be banished from the community on the other—these were the options confronting Anne Hutchinson in November, 1637, as she faced the Court in the chill of the Newton meetinghouse. The choice very likely struck her as ironic. Three years ago she had come for the same reasons as her accusers did—to escape God's impending judgment on England and to "help raise and support" the church of the new colony "while it is in the bud and infancy of its life," as Winthrop had put it in his recruiting pamphlet, the "General Observations." She had joined the Boston church where John Cotton ministered as the official teacher. She had worked tirelessly to assist women of Boston in treating their sick families. She had assisted many of them during labor and childbirth. She had helped many in the community to "enquire more seriously after the Lord Jesus Christ," as even John Winthrop had to admit. She had begun holding meetings in her house—the very ones which the court had only recently condemned—to prevent her friends and neighbors from thinking she was "proud." She had done such things precisely to become "profitable" to the Boston church and community. Yet in November 1637, she faced the threat of exile. How had such altruistic actions brought her to so stark a choice?

Anne Hutchinson's trial culminated a pitched struggle which had raged for nearly two years over the theology which would define the new community and the discipline which would order it. The roots of the conflict trace back to different expectations which various colonists had envisioned for Massachusetts Bay. The puritanism of the Bay Colony's inhabitants, according to the most recent scholarship, was not the unified, tightly constructed system it has often been thought. To be sure, most colonists shared a Calvinist framework to which they rallied as Laudian opposition intensified in the 1620s and 1630s. Yet the puritans' united front against anti-Calvinism masked subtle differences in theology. The political and ecclesiastical constraints they faced in England limited their ability to express their differing ideas and to try them out in practice.

In New England, however, Laud and his bishops were three thousand miles away, giving the colonists ample freedom to experiment. The charter of the Massachusetts Bay Company, which provided a broad outline for the new colony's government, left many details of implementation to the discretion of company officers. Royal officials had never been overly concerned with such vagueness in the charters of colonial enterprises because most colonial boards remained in London, where they could be monitored. The Massachusetts Bay Company's decision to run the colony from America, however, made it very difficult for officials to interfere. They enjoyed unprecedented leeway in deciding how best to organize colonial government, how to distribute land, and how to order community life. Similarly, the absence of a bishop in America allowed ministers and people to explore forms of church organization and worship which would follow more closely patterns they detected in the Bible itself.

Within a very short time, these circumstances exposed significant differences among the colonists, many of which they had failed to recognize while in England or did not fully understand. Colonists from different English localities differed over such matters as how to organize farms, apportion land, and divide inheritances. Ministers and people discovered differences in their interpretations of scriptural texts concerning forms of worship and expressions of spiritual life. Adaptations to the New World environment quickly began to distinguish certain features of New England life from the ways they had known at home. As successive waves of migrants arrived, they encountered patterns of community life which were familiar in some ways but jarringly different in others. They also brought new ideas or emphases about such matters as church organization, Christian living, or the proper response to ceremonies—ideas stimulated by the rapidly changing political and ecclesiastical situation in England. This made early Massachusetts a scene of intense ferment, with great potential for both creative community building, and for eventual conflict over the results.

By the time the Hutchinsons arrived in 1634, Boston was four years old. The town had begun almost by accident in the weeks after John Winthrop's fleet dropped anchor at Salem in June of 1630. The Company had originally planned to settle there where a town was already established. The site "pleased them not," however, and they began searching for alternatives. An exploratory party, led by Governor Winthrop, found a site along the Mystic River which emptied into Massachusetts Bay. Deputy Governor Thomas Dudley, however, advocated an alternative location on the neighboring Charles River. The sea-weary colonists set up a temporary camp at Charlestown, on the narrow peninsula separating the two rivers, and waited for their leaders to decide. While debate dragged on, disease—primarily scurvy and dysentery or "bloody flux"—broke out and spread rapidly through the crowded, unsanitary camp. To prevent further sickness and death, the leaders decided to disperse the colonists, each prominent leader taking a group to a separate site in the Bay area. During the month of September, seven towns were founded—Watertown, Roxbury, Dorchester, Medford, Saugus, Charlestown, and Shawmut that was soon renamed Boston after the Lincolnshire town where John Cotton had served many years as minister.

Governor Winthrop's association with the town of Boston helped ensure its eventual emergence as the Bay Colony's chief town and seat of government. The town also had some natural advantages. Its location on a peninsula jutting into the bay placed Boston in a central location relative to the surrounding towns, and Beacon Hill at the peninsula's center provided a commanding view of the approach from the Atlantic. From this hill they could spot approaching vessels from a distance and buy time to prepare for attack if necessary. The peninsula's Great Cove also provided an excellent deep water harbor for docking vessels from European and New World ports. During the next year, the inhabitants laid out the town and began the process of assigning land, building houses, planting crops, and organizing a church.

Religion played a central role in Boston's organization from the very beginning. Massachusetts Bay Colony's central purpose, John Winthrop had declared on the eve of departure for New England, was to establish a "godly commonwealth" whose inhabitants could "improve our lives to do more service to the Lord" and to contribute to the "increase of the body of Christ whereof we are members." To pursue this goal, colonial leaders adapted the vague charter and formed an annually elected representative government, which held a combination of legislative and judicial powers. The charter, however, made no provision for local government of the towns which sprang up during the early months of settlement. In the absence of alternative institutions, the local churches quickly began to fill that role just as the parish system had done in England.

Several important questions confronted the colonists as they began to organize churches according to what they understood as a more biblical pattern. Primary among them was the issue of what qualified a candidate for full membership in a church. Membership included the rights to present children for baptism and to participate in the Lord's Supper. Male members could also share in decision making and serve as lay officers. Back home, virtually all of the monarch's subjects had been considered members of the Church of England by virtue of their baptism and subsequent confirmation. This policy, however, had allowed well-known hypocrites to participate as if they were sincere Christians. Merchants who cheated their customers or men who cheated their wives often brought their corrupt points of view onto decision-making lay councils in the church. Sworn enemies received Communion together as if there was nothing amiss. Parents without a shred of personal spirituality presented their children for baptism.

Puritan New Englanders believed that the New Testament upheld a higher standard of church membership. They agreed that at minimum, full membership required conscious expression of orthodox faith. It required of each candidate a promise which bound her or him to live in holy community, to pursue exemplary habits of life, and to observe the sacraments of Baptism and Communion. It required personal discipline to pursue such means of grace as personal prayer, Bible reading, and sermon attendance. It also required candidates to submit themselves to the scrutiny of fellow church members who could encourage them to remain faithful in these duties and could call their attention to any lapse.

A second issue concerned the connection between the new colonial congregations and the Church of England. This question impinged on a variety of important issues, one of the most important being how to install pastors. In England, a minister received his ordination from his bishop, and carried it with him from one church to the next. If colonists rejected—as most did—this Episcopal model of ordination, what made a minister different from any other member of a congregation? What gave him his authority? Could a minister's authority over one congregation simply transfer to another, or did each congregation have to reauthorize him to preach in the new setting? For that matter, how should each congregation be related to the others? Should all unite under an overarching governmental structure as in England or the Netherlands? Should a body of church officials oversee each congregation, as in the Presbyterian system, or should each congregation remain formally independent, linked only by ties of Christian love, and subject only to the "loving advice" of the others?

The colonists of Boston, like those of other New England towns, began to adopt the latter "congregational" model of church organization as a matter of practical necessity as well as scriptural conviction, even as debate over most questions persisted. While the colonists were still camping in Charleston, Governor Winthrop and Deputy Governor Dudley joined Reverend John Wilson and another colonial leader, Isaac Johnson, in drawing up a church covenant. By signing it, the four promised "to walke in all our wayes according to the Rule of the Gospell, and in all sincere Conformity to His holy Ordinances, and in mutuall love, and respect each to other, so neere as God shall give us grace." The four charter members then began interviewing candidates for membership and admitting those they determined were "fitly qualified" by their confession of faith and their reputation for godly living. Many of these individuals formed the core of the Boston church when Winthrop's party moved across the bay to Shawmut in September of 1630. Given the puritan composition of Boston's original population, the great majority of the town's inhabitants were eventually admitted into membership, a pattern that continued throughout the 1630s. Male heads of households could vote in church affairs, giving ordinary Bostonians a voice that naturally extended to most of the town's affairs.

Over the next four years, Boston and other New England towns took shape under the collective direction of the inhabitants. Townspeople convened to organize their communities through meetings much like the parish-wide gatherings they had known in England. They allotted land, laid out streets, set the town watch, and agreed on how to manage mundane affairs, such as removal of refuse and control of domestic animals. They built a meetinghouse near the center of the town to house both church and civil gatherings. The latter included meetings of the town, regular sessions of the Governor and his Court of

Assistants, and local courts of justice presided over by one of the Assistants acting as a local magistrate—usually one who lived in that particular community. The poorer townspeople built shacks or wigwams to shelter their families during the first winter and eventually replaced them with more permanent one-room wooden cottages roofed with thatch. The houses of more prosperous colonists differed mainly by size and number of rooms, though the merchant William Coddington built Boston's first brick house in 1632. Governor Winthrop's house was large enough to be called a "mansion" by the time it was sold in 1643, but it remained a spare, wood-frame structure much like the houses around it.

Boston's weathered houses and muddy streets often shocked new arrivals with their "meanness," yet the settlement's outward appearance belied an underlying civil and spiritual discipline among the puritan colonists which newcomers quickly embraced. Anne Hutchinson's fellow voyager William Bartholomew recalled overhearing her exclaim as their vessel "came within sight of Boston" in 1634 that "if she had not a sure word that England should be destroyed her heart would shake." A few years prior, her contemporary Anne Dudley Bradstreet had written that her own heart had "risen" in revulsion against the "new world and new manners" she encountered in the town. Yet, like most arrivals, both soon "became convinced it was the way of God," as Bradstreet put it, and became vital members of the Boston church and community.

The Hutchinson family wasted little time in building a new life in Boston. Their arrival on September 18, 1634 marked a reunion with many friends, neighbors, and acquaintances from Lincolnshire who helped to establish them in their new home. William's status as a prosperous merchant made him an especially welcome addition for his relative wealth and extensive commercial contacts as well as for the prestige he brought to the colony. Hutchinson's gentry pedigree also lent weight to the Hutchinson family's status in Boston, as did her skills in healing and midwifery. William's experience as a local officeholder in Alford also recommended him as a promising colonial leader.

William and Anne selected a building plot and began to build what was likely one of the largest houses in town. Necessity

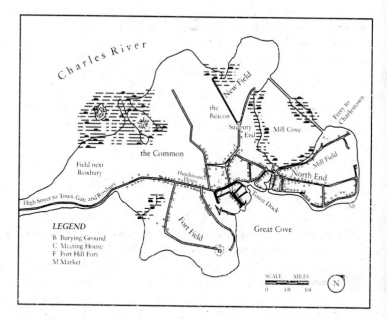

Map 3-1 Boston, c. 1635.

would have dictated the size of their new dwelling perhaps more than ostentation: besides themselves, Anne and William needed the space to house at least ten of their eleven children, and perhaps as many as five other adults. Their oldest son, Edward, had arrived the year before at the age of 21 and may have lived elsewhere. The four teenagers—Richard (19), Faith (17), Bridget (15), and Francis (14) —may have found temporary quarters with extended family or friends as they waited for the completion of their new house. After all, the Hutchinson family network in Massachusetts was quite large, eventually numbering 38 people. The other adults of the household—Anne's sister Katherine Marbury, two of William's cousins Anne and Francis Freiston, and the two servants, John Hord and Edward Dennis—may have done likewise. For shelter the first winter, William and Anne likely dug a cellar which they lined and roofed with wooden planks for themselves and the six younger children—Sammy (10), Anne (8), Mary (6), Katherine (4), William (3), and Susanna (1).

The Hutchinsons' choice of Boston may have been influenced by the presence there of John Cotton, who had arrived in September of 1633. The Boston church had welcomed Cotton with open arms, but even his prestige as one of England's most distinguished preachers did not exempt him from submitting to the church's process of membership. Indeed, Cotton himself insisted upon it. John Winthrop recorded in his diary that on the Saturday after their arrival, Cotton "made his Confession according to order" and was "admitted a member" along with his wife, Sarah. Once admitted, they immediately presented their infant son Seaborn for baptism by Reverend John Wilson. The following month, the congregation held a fast to ordain Cotton as "Teacher of the Congregation of Boston," where Wilson continued to serve as pastor. To Hutchinson, the opportunity to sit under Cotton's teaching represented no less than the fulfillment of a prophecy she had received in England that "thine eyes shall see thy teachers."

Anne and William underwent the same membership process several weeks after their arrival. William made a satisfactory confession of faith and was admitted on October 26, 1634, but Pastor Wilson later reported that "there was some difficulty made" about Anne's suitability for membership. During her passage across the Atlantic, she had expressed disagreement with Reverend Zechariah Symmes over the interpretation of John 13:35, "by this shall all men know that ye are my disciples, if ye have love one to another." Symmes had preached to the ship's passengers that their "love of the brethren" constituted one piece of evidence that they had been chosen by God for salvation. Hutchinson challenged Symmes's interpretation with several biblical quotations, including Jesus' declaration to his disciples that "I have many things to say but you cannot bear them now." This quotation from John 16:12 introduces Jesus' teaching concerning the future ministry of the Holy Spirit, and Hutchinson's use of it suggests that she was claiming to have a clearer understanding than Symmes of how God gave assurance of salvation. When the ship arrived in Boston, the offended Symmes complained about the "corruptness and narrowness of her opinions" to Thomas Dudley, the elected governor in 1634 and a member of the Boston church. Dudley invited Symmes to attend Anne Hutchinson's membership interview, where he could voice his concerns to the church leadership.

In doing so, Symmes became the first to call public attention to Anne Hutchinson's unusual views on how Christians obtained assurance—confidence that they were true believers and members of the elect. Teacher Cotton took Reverend Symmes's misgivings seriously and questioned Hutchinson carefully during her membership interview. Pastor Wilson had returned to England not long before her interview to assist in further recruitment efforts, but he later recalled from reports that her responses to Symmes's concerns satisfied the Boston church leadership that her views were acceptable. She admitted to Cotton and the Boston church leaders that expressions of "sanctification" such as "love of the brethren" could indeed provide assurance that a person had been truly justified—made righteous by God as one of his chosen people. She asserted only that the inward *experience* of assurance came first, a point which the Boston church leaders "did not greatly stand upon."

Indeed, Wilson and Cotton themselves disagreed over the issue which Hutchinson had raised, as did other church members. As we have seen, Cotton believed that assurance rested more firmly on the Spirit's inner witness than on evidence gleaned from a holy life or sanctification. Wilson, on the other hand, held the more standard sanctificationist view that holy dispositions and actions also offered reliable evidence for assurance. The two nevertheless shared a very effective ministry together. The view Hutchinson expressed during her membership interview echoed Cotton's rather than Wilson's, but Cotton expressed hope that Hutchinson would follow his example of harmonious cooperation with Wilson by "holding with us in that truth [sanctification as evidence of assurance] as well as the other."

Symmes's concerns produced a brief delay in Anne Hutchinson's admission while the members considered her case. Yet she soon took her seat in the meetinghouse with her family and alongside other members with whom she may well have disagreed. Anne's admission was recorded the week after William's. Four teenaged children, Richard, Faith, Bridget, and Francis, were also admitted by the end of December. A fifth, 22-year-old Edward, had been admitted soon after his arrival the previous year.

The flap over Anne Hutchinson's views did little to dampen her family's welcome during the next two years. Both husband and wife quickly assumed leading roles in the community. William was soon collaborating with other Boston merchants to strengthen the colony's commerce, aided by his family connections in London and Lincolnshire. In March 1635, he was administered the "freeman's oath" along with his sons Richard and Francis. This gave all three the right to vote in the colony's annual elections, as well as making them eligible to hold office. Indeed, according to the Massachusetts Bay Company charter, the body of the freemen held full power to legislate for the colony—a level of political power unknown to freeholders in England.

Two months after William Hutchinson became a freeman, the people of Boston elected him to serve as one of the town's two "deputies" in a newly reorganized General Court. The office of deputy had been created only the previous May in recognition of the fact that a legislature composed of every single freeman was impractical in the rapidly growing colony. The colonists contented themselves with assembling as a body only once each May to elect the governor and his eighteen Assistants. For the other three meetings of the year, the freemen of the towns sent two deputies each to represent their interests in the General Court, the colony's main legislative body. Hutchinson's election to this important post provides a gauge of his status as well as the confidence he had won among his fellow townspeople in such a short time. He was also soon elected to the local offices of town selectman—an office similar to alderman or city council member—as well as a petty magistrate or local judge and a deacon of the church.

As a colonial officeholder in both church and state, William Hutchinson participated directly in the development of what historians have called the "culture of discipline" in early New England. The General Court exercised both its legislative and judicial functions to encourage communal harmony, while prohibiting and punishing behavior considered harmful to colony's moral and spiritual life. Magistrates dealt severely with criminal activity such as theft, assault, and murder, but they also legislated and enforced a rigorous moral code. As Winthrop had said in his *Model of Christian Charity* sermon, colonists had made a covenant with God to "improve our lives to do more in service to the Lord." The responsibility for keeping this pact extended far beyond the doors of the meetinghouse. Colonial leaders held a moral duty to set an example of godly living before one another and the colony's children, and to ensure that no colonist undercut that example by his or her own public misbehavior.

This disciplinary function of colonial government meant that William Hutchinson may have meted out many punishments for offenses which today would seem strange, intrusive, and downright shocking. If a father decided to take his sons hunting or played a sport with them on Sunday, he could be fined or whipped for Sabbath-breaking. A man or a woman who slandered a neighbor might also be fined and whipped. If the slander was vicious enough, the convicted party might have a portion of his ears cut off or even be banished from the colony. If a man had too much to drink, he would be much better off staying over at a neighbor's to sleep it off. If he was caught a first time walking home drunk in public, he could find himself spending time in the stocks, with a sign posted labeling him a drunkard. If caught a second or third time, he might face disfranchisement—losing the right to vote—and might have to wear a large "D" around his neck for a year or longer. A young couple who lost control of their passion and had sex before marriage could be fined and whipped for fornication. Adultery carried the death penalty, though this was rarely enforced. Puritans believed that God had created sex for enjoyment as well as procreation, but only within the covenant of marriage. A person caught carrying cards or dice or even smoking in public could be fined. A merchant who charged too much for his goods could face prosecution. Indeed, William Hutchinson himself served on a committee of the General Court to investigate and propose solutions to price-gouging in Massachusetts during the summer of 1635.

As a member and leader in the Boston church, William Hutchinson would have participated in dispensing church discipline as well. A member who committed an infraction of civil law could also incur congregational discipline. This often entailed a public humiliation—a confession of sin along with a heartfelt expression of repentance. Cases of conflict between church members could result in opponents being suspended from participation in the Lord's Supper until they achieved reconciliation. Extreme moral lapses could result in excommunication—ejection from membership, permanent exclusion from participation in the Lord's Supper, and loss of the right to present children for baptism.

Wherever possible, New England leaders sought to prevent the need for such punishments by encouraging positive discipline in the practice of good works and mutual care, an effort in which the churches played a leading role. Ministers and magistrates urged neighbors to watch over each other, to encourage one another in cultivating godly lives. Neighbors should express "love of the brethren" in practical ways, helping a sick mother by tending the children and bringing over meals, helping an injured farmer to harvest his crops, joining the family down the road in tracking down their pigs or rounding up their cows. This formed an important basis for establishing systems of poor relief in the towns: care for a community's poor demonstrated Christian charity and removed a common incentive for covetousness, theft, and disorder. Church members who committed thoughtless offenses or broke into disagreement were encouraged to clear the air early on in private conversation. They should not allow the conflict to mushroom into a problem which would require formal intervention by church elders or local magistrates. In England this concern for intervening in the conduct of others had earned the puritan a reputation as nosy, self-righteous busybodies, but many families in early Massachusetts welcomed the sincere concern of neighbors for their spiritual well-being.

Church elders and civil magistrates confronted all but the most incorrigible moral offenders with the goal of restoring them into harmonious relations with the church and community, though they differed on whether severity or leniency was more effective. In his capacity as a magistrate, Thomas Dudley tended to hew to the letter of the law and frequently accused his rival John Winthrop of excessive leniency. Winthrop did indeed defend a more merciful approach. When dealing with conflict, for example, he labored to "improve that which is profitable," finding and incorporating the best points of each side, while overlooking harsh words or abrasive conduct by "cover[ing] the rest with love."

Anne Hutchinson excelled at providing the spiritual encouragement and works of mercy which constituted the positive side of Boston's culture of discipline. As a gentlewoman by birth and the matron of a leading family, she assumed a position of respect and leadership among the women of the town. Her skills in healing and midwifery further enhanced her esteem, even though the town of Boston had already named Goodwife Jane Hawkins as its official midwife. Labor and childbirth was hazardous for both mothers and infants in the early modern world, and skilled midwives earned gratitude and respect from the women who benefitted from their services. The occupation also carried religious significance, both from biblical examples and from the opportunity to offer spiritual counsel to women in labor. Puritan midwives claimed the Old Testament heroes Shiphrah and Puah as their models—two biblical midwives who earned praise for refusing Pharaoh's order to kill male Hebrew infants near the time of the Exodus. Some evidence suggests that English Catholics and Protestants each regarded midwives as important front-line agents in the clandestine war between the two faiths because of their access to infants at the moment of birth. Catholic midwives were suspected of secretly administering "popish" baptisms to the newborns they delivered. As a result, English midwives often had to swear licensing oaths, which included a promise not to allow any child they delivered to be baptized "by any Mass-Latine, service or other prayers than such as are appointed by the laws of the church of England."

Hutchinson's ability to assist at childbirth gave her the chance to build a large social network very quickly. Childbirth in early New England was a community affair, drawing female family, friends, and neighbors to the expectant mother's house to offer encouragement and practical support. A woman in the last stages of pregnancy entered a period of "confinement" which began in the days or weeks just prior to birth, and continued for nearly a month afterward. During this period her household filled with conversation and bustled with activity as friends and family assumed the household duties. This was intended to allow the expectant mother to conserve her strength for labor and to regain it once the child was born. The presence of so many women in the house provided a chance for old acquaintances to deepen friendships, and new arrivals to become acquainted with their neighbors while proving their worth through acts of service. The women of the community took turns caring for the mother's children, cooking for her family, and tending to her housework. They exchanged advice on marriage and child care.

Hutchinson could speak to such matters from long experience. She had endured fourteen childbirths during her twenty-three years of marriage, and eleven of those children had lived to accompany her to America. As she ministered to other expectant mothers during 1635–1636 she was pregnant again, lending even greater credibility to the advice she gave. "She was a woman of good wit," her brother-in-law John Wheelwright later remembered, "but naturally of a good judgement too." Wheelwright recalled that she frequently demonstrated these virtues in her acts of public service such as attending women at childbirth.

Hutchinson's neighborliness and skill in healing and midwifery opened the door for her to provide spiritual counsel to women in labor "and other occasios of bodily infirmities." John Cotton later recalled that as she ably assisted Goodwife Hawkins "in womans meeting at Chilbirth-Travells," she was adept at turning the conversation to spiritual matters. The uncertainties and fears accompanying labor made childbirth a time of great spiritual sensitivity both for the new mother herself and for the women attending her. Were their own souls really secure? If they died during childbirth, would they be with God or would they be forever lost in the torments of Hell? Were they sincere Christians themselves, truly fit to present their newborns for baptism, or were they deceiving themselves? Did they possess the spiritual resources necessary to teach their babies about God's ways as they grew, to help their children find salvation? Hutchinson was skilled at drawing out such fears in conversation, helping many to discern that they had in fact based their assurance of eternal salvation solely on their external practice of good habits of life. They had "gone on in a Covenant of Works." They had never paused to consider that their private prayer, their family Bible reading, their faithful attendance at weekly church services, their respect for ministers, their attention to sermons and lectures, their self-discipline and honesty—all these might be nothing more than "common gifts and graces" shared by many apparently good people who had never experienced true grace. "Shaken and humbled" by the realization that they had been relying only on their good deeds to get them to heaven, many of the women Hutchinson counseled began "to enquire more seriously after the Lord Jesus Christ."

John Cotton welcomed Hutchinson's "private conferences" while attending women in childbirth, believing that they echoed his own public preaching concerning assurance and the Covenant of Grace. Indeed, several women reported that their conversations with Hutchinson "awakened" them to the realization that they had been deceiving themselves about the security of their spiritual condition. She helped them to understand what it meant to exercise sincere faith in Jesus and to experience true conversion. Having learned the folly of seeking signs of her own assurance of election in her good works, Hutchinson was able to encourage other women to more reliable evidence of their assurance in the inner "witnesse of the Spirit." This proven skill at providing spiritual counsel won her universal praise from members of the Boston church, who "blessed God for her fruitfull discourses."

Hutchinson's growing reputation as a gifted counselor of souls prompted women to seek her out for spiritual advice, a fact other Bostonians probably found unsurprising during her first two years in Boston. The practice of lay counseling was already well established in England, often encouraged by the ministers themselves as an important part of puritan spiritual discipline. Hutchinson was by no means the first puritan English woman to exercise such a gift. Since the time of Protestant persecution under Mary I and probably before, puritan women had provided spiritual encouragement and engaged in theological debate with lay people and even ordained clergy. Seventeenth-century lay women such as Briget Cooke encouraged others to come to her for spiritual counsel. Indeed, at least one female prophet, Anne Fenwick, was able in 1629 to publish a volume of Scriptural promises selected to provide encouragement to puritan readers. Puritan male peers often accepted the ability of such women to provide spiritual encouragement since women were thought especially receptive to the Holy Spirit's influence.

Hutchinson's neighborliness and skill in ministering to body and soul contributed to a broader climate of spiritual excitement in Boston and the other towns of the Massachusetts Bay Colony in 1635. Looking back on this period in the years after her trial, even a critic so hostile as John Winthrop commented that her spiritual counsel at this time consisted of "wholesome truths" which "all the faithful imbraced." The colony was in the middle of a growth spurt, which by 1636 would double its population from the 3,000 who inhabited the towns the year the Hutchinson family arrived. New colonists found in the churches of Massachusetts the embodiment of their hopes for a biblical, truly Reformed commonwealth liberated from the trappings of a corrupt ecclesiastical establishment. Many learned puritan ministers were populating the pulpits of Massachusetts with the kind of lively preaching rapidly being silenced by Laudian bishops back home. Ministers established weekday lectures as well—two per week in Boston—offering up a feast of sermons and Bible teaching to people who had been forced to trudge a distance of twenty miles or more to hear the like in England. John Cotton himself saw Hutchinson's activities during this time as an important element of Boston's spiritual vitality, observing that throughout her first two years in the colony, she served as a faithful partner with the ministers in performing "the work of the Lord."

This atmosphere of spiritual excitement also encompassed significant diversity of viewpoints, which the colonists managed to tolerate well into 1636. To be sure, the range of views remained largely confined within the boundaries of Reformed Protestantism. Even so, differences which might seem minor to an outsider could easily fracture a community whose members refused to extend patience and forbearance to each other. John Cotton and John Wilson modeled such mutual toleration from the same Boston pulpit and readily extended it to members such as Anne Hutchinson who differed from each of them. Differing parties consciously recognized disparities in their views and addressed them on occasion. Cotton, for instance, warned Hutchinson of his concern that she tended to disregard sermons and lectures to rely too much on her own private devotional life, strengthening her faith not by attending public preaching and worship, but "by private Meditations, or Revelations onely." Other church members exercised discretion concerning their differences with Cotton and Wilson, and with one another. After all, as the historian Michael Winship has pointed out, they had hazarded an Atlantic crossing to become part of this new puritan colony, and they did not want a few minor differences of opinion to prevent them from enjoying its rich spiritual benefits. Persons who held differing theological views were often content to differ "in a spirit of Christian meekness and love" until "God may be pleased to manifest his Trueth" to one or the other.

Members of the various churches of the Bay Colony were also able to detect differences among the ministers as they visited other towns to attend weekday lectures or spend time with family or friends. The ministers corresponded and visited each other to seek advice and correction which would prevent their straying off into dangerous doctrinal territory. Colonial magistrates such as Winthrop and Dudley frequently attended such meetings as well, often speaking or "prophesying" as lay preachers and participating in discussions. Winthrop, for example, once halted a debate between Cotton and the Salem magistrate John Endicott when he perceived them "growing to some earnestness" over whether or not Scripture required women to wear veils in public.

The case of the fiery young minister Roger Williams illustrates both the extraordinary patience of the colony's puritan authorities and the limits of toleration. Williams repeatedly tested the patience of Massachusetts ministers and magistrates by advocating extreme points of view in religious and even civil matters. Soon after his arrival in Boston in 1631, Williams sparked controversy by refusing to join the congregation because they "would not make public declaration of their repentance for having Communion with the Churches of Englande while they liued there." In response, the churches and the General Court warned the nearby Salem congregation not to call Williams as their minister as they had planned to do. Williams subsequently left for the Separatist colony of Plymouth, whose leaders had made a formal break with the Church of England. In 1633, however, he returned to Salem after concluding that the Pilgrim colony had not proved Separate enough for him. There he once again incurred the General Court's censure for, among other things, "charging King Iames with a solemn public lye" because the Royal patent claimed that "he was the first Christian Prince that had discovered this land." For the next two years, Williams persistently advocated what the General Court considered "diverse dangerous opinions" from his home in Salem. Finally in 1635, the magistrates' patience was exhausted, and they sentenced him to be sent back to England. Before the sentence could be carried out, however, John Winthrop warned Williams, who fled to Narragansett Bay.

Anne Hutchinson observed, experienced, and likely reveled in this welter of diversity from her home in Boston. Her husband

William sat as deputy in the General Court of 1635 which banished Roger Williams, probably making the matter a topic of dinner conversation as the case unfolded. Hutchinson attended public lectures of visiting ministers as well as those of Cotton and Wilson where she compared and critiqued their doctrine and preaching style. Without a doubt, Hutchinson must have begun to form private opinion concerning the relative approaches the various Bay colony ministers took to the Covenant of Grace. Yet no evidence suggests that she made any unfavorable public comparison between other ministers and her respected teacher John Cotton until sometime in the spring or summer of 1636. Every surviving testimony indicates that she threw her heart and soul into becoming a "profitable member" among Boston's inhabitants.

In March 1636, Hutchinson entered her own period of confinement to deliver her latest son Zuriel. Her "brother Wheelwright" later recalled that during these times "many strange fancies, and erroneous tenents possest her." He drew on common medical theory of the day to explain this phenomenon, attributing it to the poor "quality of humors" or bodily fluids which affected health and mental disposition. Wheelwright also thought that the devil himself was at work. Hutchinson's condition made her melancholy, giving Satan an opening opportunity to afflict her with delusions. Wheelwright's assessment of Hutchinson's symptoms were likely shared by the women of the community, who reciprocated her earlier charity toward many of them by gathering at her home to tend her children and keep her household. Wheelwright's description of Hutchinson's "melancholy" suggests to the modern reader that she may have been suffering from some degree of postpartum depression, a condition with which her friends would have been familiar. Whatever the nature of her affliction, they sought to lift her spirits by engaging her in prayer, psalm singing, and godly conversation.

Hutchinson's strength returned sufficiently for her to emerge from confinement no later than the end of April 1636. By that time, a chain of events had begun in Boston that would soon entangle her and set her on a course toward exile. Massachusetts' greatest crisis to date, the controversy over free grace and assurance, was about to begin.

Secret Quarrels

"I would go a little higher with Mrs. Hutchinson," Deputy Governor Thomas Dudley declared midway through the first day of her trial in November 1637. *"About three years ago we were all in peace,"* he recalled, but *"Mrs. Hutchinson from that time she came hath made a disturbance."* The first hint of trouble had appeared as soon as she arrived, when *"some that came with her in the ship"* complained about Hutchinson's views. John Cotton had managed temporarily to satisfy Dudley *"that she held nothing different from us"* during her interview for church membership. Yet *"within half a year after,"* the deputy governor continued, *"she had vented divers of her strange opinions and had made parties in the country."* Eventually Dudley came to believe that *"Mr. Cotton and [Sir Henry] Vane were of her judgment, but Mr. Cotton hath since cleared himself that he was not of that mind."* Even so, he observed, *"this women's meeting"* at the Hutchinson house had enabled Hutchinson to create a *"potent party in the country"* which *"endangered"* the puritan commonwealth. Anne Hutchinson had become a powerful symbolic figure of the views which formed the *"foundation"* of this party, Dudley reasoned. The Court had only to *"take away the foundation,"* Hutchinson herself, *"and the building will fall."*

Dudley's speech provides a neatly constructed summary of Anne Hutchinson's activities in Boston as told by those who judged her at the time. For centuries Dudley's speech has also shaped how her story has been told by historians and biographers. Its frequent retelling has made Hutchinson the architect of a powerful, unified opposition movement, whose foundations she subtly began to lay even before she arrived in Boston. Her "strange opinions" formed the building blocks of this movement and her weekly meetings the tool. With them she "traduced the ministers and magistrates," undermining their authority and threatening the colony with anarchy. She was, in John Winthrop's words, the "breeder and nourisher of all these distempers," the "old root" out of which sprang the "young branches" of what later historians have labeled "Hutchinsonian" dissent.

A closer look at how events unfolded after the spring of 1636 suggests that this old familiar story is a bit too neat. In the first place, Dudley's own memory was faulty. As the previous chapter has suggested, Hutchinson lived as a "profitable member" among the townspeople of Boston for nearly two years. Only in October 1636 did Winthrop record an entry in his journal mentioning any trouble involving her. To be sure, he may have observed the comings and goings at her house that summer with mounting concern. Yet the best evidence suggests that prior to the birth of her baby boy Zuriel, and indeed for some months after, the people of Boston still regarded Hutchinson a welcome and valuable contributor to the community. Furthermore, Winthrop's same journal entry suggests that John Cotton, teacher of the Boston church, aroused at least as much concern as Hutchinson did for reportedly teaching that "no sanctification can help to evidence to us our justification."

In contrast to Dudley's portrayal of Anne Hutchinson as an inveterate rabble-rouser from the time she landed in Boston, the evidence suggests that "secret quarrels," according to newcomer Thomas Shepard, began tugging at the fabric of Boston's famous unity only during the late spring and summer of 1636 while Hutchinson was recovering from her most recent childbirth. Historians have long noted the formation of at least two factions over the question of assurance and free grace: a "Free Grace" party which rallied around John Cotton's insistence on the "witness of the Spirit" for assurance and what we have termed a "sanctificationist" party which based assurance on evidence drawn from a sincere convert's life of faith. Such differences had existed in the colony for several years but had never caused division, thanks to the townspeople's mutual forbearance and Cotton's and Winthrop's efforts to preserve unity and love.

Anne Hutchinson certainly played a leading role in the development of these factions, although the historian Michael Winship has recently argued that she did not do so alone. Between 1635 and 1636, three influential leaders arrived in the colony who did not share Cotton's conciliatory temperament or Winthrop's tolerance of a range of viewpoints on free grace and assurance. Sir Henry Vane, the younger son of a privy councilor to Charles I himself, brought to Massachusetts an activism and a passion for speculation in religious matters. He quickly became an energetic champion of free grace. Reverend John Wheelwright, Anne Hutchinson's brother-in-law, coupled free grace views with an impetuosity more suited to aggravating than calming conflict. On the other side of the free grace issue, the sanctificationist Reverend Thomas Shepard brought with him a determination to search out deviant teaching and eradicate it. Wheelwright has figured prominently in the historical record, but the contrasting roles played by Vane and Shepard have been obscured. This has shaped the subsequent telling of Anne Hutchinson's story. Yet the influence of both Vane and Shepard is crucial to understanding why Hutchinson abandoned her earlier willingness to temper her views, and instead began making a "potent party in the country" through her weekly meetings.

Sir Henry Vane's arrival in Boston must have captivated Anne Hutchinson and her family as much as it did most other colonists of Massachusetts Bay. Born to wealth and power and a member of the royal court, he was the most important English figure to come to the colony during its founding years. His father, also named Henry, had provided a fitting education which included the prestigious Westminster School, a period at Magdalen Hall, Oxford, and travel to Paris as well as the great centers of Continental Protestantism at Geneva and Leiden. The year he turned eighteen, Sir Henry's father used his extensive diplomatic connections to gain his son a six-month appointment as aid to the English ambassador in Vienna. There the younger Vane distinguished himself for his keen insight, "discreet discourse" and "comely fashion." Yet he also distinguished himself in zeal for the godly Protestantism which had gripped him during a dramatic conversion experience a few years earlier, a distinction which did not sit well at court. When he resolved to sail to Massachusetts Bay in 1635, Charles and Laud both gave their blessing in the hope that the time he spent with the godly there would grate on his courtly sensibilities and so cure him of his puritanism.

The colonists eagerly welcomed the twenty-two-year-old Vane into the religious and political life of Massachusetts Bay. John Cotton made space for Vane in his own home, and eventually added on a lean-to for the young gentleman's use. The Boston church admitted Vane to membership on November 1, 1635. At the end of that month the Boston town meeting passed an order requiring that any colonists considering a lawsuit should first seek arbitration through Vane and panel of two church elders. In early January the young statesman employed his diplomatic skills to arbitrate Thomas Dudley's and John Winthrop's longstanding feud over the relative strictness of colonial government. The meeting he convened for this purpose culminated not only in a "renewal of love" among the assembled ministers and magistrates, but also in the adoption of ten articles resolving to pursue "more strictness in . . . Civil Government and military discipline" in a spirit of greater public unity. Finally, in May, 1636, the freeholders of Massachusetts rewarded Vane for his early contributions to the colony's political life by electing him governor.

Vane's early efforts to reconcile the rift between Winthrop and Dudley suggested that he might improve and further extend the unity which Boston and the rest of the colony had celebrated in the early years. Yet in the rarified air of a godly commonwealth where he could "enjoy the ordinances of God in their purity," Vane soon began to experiment with theological ideas once again. Indeed, his early efforts to promote godly colonial unity expressed a visionary desire to reconstruct society on the principles of the New Testament. Vane's zeal and idealism ultimately undercut the atmosphere of moderation which had, so far, enabled ministers and lay people to overcome their theological differences with love.

Sir Henry Vane apparently recognized Anne Hutchinson as an ally in the pursuit of free grace because of her well-known influence among the women of Boston as well as her devotion to his host John Cotton's teaching. According to John Winthrop, her decision to "open her house to all comers" was encouraged by certain figures "of eminent place and parts"—a cautious allusion to Vane. Her own trial testimony suggests that the women of Boston also played a part in the development of her weekly meetings. They expected that a gentlewoman with such a reputation for godliness and Bible knowledge would host a gathering for prayer and discussion of the scriptures. When the women began to gossip that her delay in doing so betrayed her pride and contempt for ordinary means of grace such as prayer and Bible study, Hutchinson silenced the rumors by opening her home.

Vane's encouragement and the expectations of Hutchinson's Boston neighbors suggest that her decision to host meetings challenged no boundary of gender, or even of propriety. Indeed, her gatherings may initially have been considered a continuation of the informal conversation and community-building that had occurred around the time of Zuriel's birth. Hutchinson's meetings were certainly not the only ones held in Boston during this period, nor even the first. Such meetings were hardly illegal in Massachusetts. It was very common for family and friends to gather and discuss the minister's weekly sermon or lecture, the stated purpose of the assemblies at the Hutchinson house. The freedom to hold these gatherings would have been widely defended by godly colonists who had chafed under Laud's effort to suppress such "conventicles." Experienced, mature matrons such as Anne Hutchinson could also find precedent for leading gatherings of this sort in scriptures such as Titus 2:4, which encouraged older women to "instruct the young women." As Simon Bradstreet, a member of the General Court, remarked during Hutchinson's trial, "I am not against all women's meetings but do think them to be lawful."

Hutchinson's meetings eventually did become exceptional in at least one respect, however: their size and popularity. At their height, the meetings drew between sixty and eighty persons twice per week, roughly ten percent of Boston's adult population of six hundred. One of the meetings was open exclusively to women and Hutchinson herself presided, answering questions about the sermon, Bible doctrine, and spiritual life from her seat in a prominently placed chair. It is not clear who directed the second, which included men as well. Hutchinson denied ever leading it, and the judges at her trial eventually had to concede that she had never "crossed the rule" which forbade women to teach men. A long list of men within Hutchinson's circle would have been competent enough to lead mixed gatherings, including Governor Vane himself, her husband William Hutchinson, her brothers-in-law Edward Hutchinson and John Wheelwright, Boston church elder Thomas Leverett, and deacon John Coggeshall.

Winthrop and Dudley eventually came to see Hutchinson's meetings as the source of the radical views which divided Massachusetts, yet it seems likely that those views emerged gradually as the meetings progressed through the summer and fall of 1636. Winthrop later claimed that Hutchinson initially affirmed "wholesome truths," but later began to "set forth her own stuffe." The "wholesome truths" came from the recitation and discussion of Cotton's sermons, which formed the core of each meeting. Hutchinson apparently added her "own stuffe" through commentary. John Cotton later recalled "what she repeated and confirmed" of his sermons "was accounted sound," but anything he had said which Hutchinson did not repeat was disregarded as "Apocrypha" rather than reliable teaching. He insisted, however, that "this change of hers was long hid from me."

John Cotton's unawareness of what transpired at Hutchinson's meetings may have stemmed in part from his habit of giving parishioners the benefit of the doubt. It may also suggest that Hutchinson's ideas rarely strayed far from Cotton's own, and that whenever they did, Cotton's parishioners themselves exercised the habits of tolerance which had so far helped to preserve the unity of the Boston church. When the controversy later made its way into court, many of those who had attended her meetings refused to believe that Hutchinson and some of her friends really held the unorthodox ideas attributed to them. This suggests that she was quite cautious in airing her opinions and that what she said in her meetings varied little from either Cotton's views or those of her listeners. Others such as her "brother Wheelwright" recognized that Hutchinson's usual good judgment might be clouded at times by her habit of giving "her understanding over into the power of suggestion and immediate dictates." According to Thomas Weld, who later edited John Winthrop's *Short Story of the Rise, Reign and Ruin of the Antinomians, Familists, and Libertines*, some of those who attended the Hutchinson's meetings were "magistrates . . . scholars . . . men of learning . . . and men eminent for Religion, parts and wit." John Winthrop observed that many of these, capable as they were of exercising informed judgment concerning Bible doctrine, sought "cloakes to cover the nakedness" of any errors they detected in Hutchinson's statements. Following Winthrop's own example, they "improved" what they found "profitable" in her commentary and "covered the rest with love."

What some saw as an exercise in Christian charity, however, others perceived as too much lenience, indulgence, and even negligence. Events soon revealed that Reverend Thomas Shepard shared this view, especially concerning Hutchinson's—and even Cotton's—views concerning assurance. Shepard had arrived in Massachusetts at the same time as Sir Henry Vane in October 1635 along with a number of settlers. He soon began working with these people and others in Newtown to gather a new church there and become its pastor (the first Newtown church was preparing to move *en masse* to Connecticut the following June with their pastor and Shepard's father-in-law, Thomas Hooker). Shepard had been ejected from his lectureship in England by Laud himself in 1630. He had spent the next three years "tossed from the south to the north of England," moving clandestinely among a puritan network led by Hooker and the prominent Essex minister John Rogers. During this period he had preached wherever he could in private homes and occasional public venues while remaining constantly on the run to avoid arrest by Laud's ecclesiastical agents.

Shepard brought an expertise in diagnosing the spiritual state of souls to Massachusetts, a skill he had honed through ceaseless introspection of his own conscience for evidence of sincere faith. Additionally, he was keenly sensitive to any teaching which might deceive parishioners into basing their sense of assurance upon insufficient evidence. His biographer Michael McGiffert has described Shepard as a "warmly evangelical" pastor who "had little talent or desire for combative Nonconformity." This aspect of his personality may have held some appeal for Anne

Hutchinson, who certainly would have applauded his concern that no parishioner should mistake her own good works for evidence of faith. John Cotton recalled that of all the New England pastors other than himself, Hutchinson thought most highly of Shepard. Yet Shepard's personal warmth did little to temper his passion for a precise application of his sanctificationist views to the critical issues of faith and assurance. Indeed, most historians of the controversy have suggested that Shepard became the spokesperson for a network of ministers who shared a similar passion for doctrinal precision, including his father-in-law Thomas Hooker and an old friend, Rev. Thomas Weld of Roxbury. Shepard's insistence on doctrinal precision contradicted the kind of toleration which Cotton and Wilson had been practicing at Boston. This, coupled with his commitment to the sanctificationist view of assurance, soon set him on a collision course with John Cotton and Anne Hutchinson in spite of her regard for him.

Shepard quickly made it a hallmark of his ministry to insist on an accurate understanding and application of assurance in the Bay Colony churches. When gathering his own church in Newtown, Shepard required candidates for membership to do more than simply confess their faith and promise to uphold the church covenant. A person who wished to join Shepard's church had to find the words to "declare what work of Grace the Lord had wroughte in them," expressing their own inner experiences of grace in precise theological terms. At the founding ceremony of the Newtown church, Shepard and six other charter members modeled the kind of conversion narrative he had in mind while a delegation of ministers and representatives of the General Court watched attentively. The General Court soon passed an order requiring the similar delegations of magistrates and ministerial advisors during the formation of any new church. Shepard subsequently used his influence as an observer at such gatherings to instill theologically precise views on assurance in churches throughout the Bay Colony.

The new requirement of a conversion narrative made the process of interviewing candidates for church membership much more exacting than it had been when Winthrop and Dudley organized the first Massachusetts congregation in 1630. The colonists at that time had remained sensitive to the controversy that surrounded the notion of making true conversion a requirement for church membership. Many Reformed ministers harbored serious doubt whether even the most discerning Christian could accurately judge the experience of another's inmost heart. Many puritan clergy thought the idea smacked of Separatism by implying that the Church of England was an unacceptably impure mixture of true converts or "visible saints" and hypocrites who possessed no grounds for assurance. In recognition of this controversy, the founding churches had accepted into membership many whose expressions of faith Shepard later found sadly wanting. Shepard was dissatisfied with some members who had been received on what he regarded as inadequate or erroneous grounds. His discontent sparked new tensions which contributed to the colony's growing theological unrest.

Lay people found it difficult to frame their sense of assurance in precise theological terms which Shepard demanded. Three aspiring members of Richard Mather's Dorchester congregation discovered this when a visiting Thomas Shepard objected to their conversion accounts. Shepard charged that the three had improperly grounded their assurance too much on their own righteousness, an objection which Anne Hutchinson would certainly have approved. Yet Shepard also rejected the three because their sense of assurance relied too much on "fits and dreams," evidence Hutchinson may well have accepted if phrased in terms she approved. John Cotton remembered correcting a similar fault in Hutchinson's own sense of assurance during a private conversation with her. He had observed that her assurance was "scarce at any time strengthened, by publick Ministery, but by private Meditations, or Revelations onely."

Shepard soon carried the contest over assurance to John Cotton himself. Sometime between February and June 1636, the young minister, twenty years Cotton's junior, accompanied some of his new parishioners to one of Cotton's lectures. There they heard Cotton make several statements concerning assurance and the Christian life. Shepard found these statements unsettling and sat down early the following week to write Cotton a letter. In it, he asked the senior minister to "clear up the truth" of those statements "by way of writing rather than speech." Shepard professed concern about rumors of "secret quarrels already begun" and "seeming differences & jarrs" among the ministers, but the real target of his concern was Cotton's own teaching. Shepard made no direct mention of Anne Hutchinson or her meetings. His reference to "secret" quarrels may in fact suggest that colonial ministers and people were trying to preserve the famous unity of the colony Massachusetts by keeping their differences private—especially any between themselves and John Cotton. Shepard's letter reveals a man unwilling to play nice. He would not let the sleeping dog of perceived error lie for the sake of colonial peace.

Historians have in fact debated whether Cotton's and Anne Hutchinson's views really differed much from one another in 1636. Perhaps Shepard correctly perceived Cotton as the true source of Hutchinson's controversial views concerning free grace, and Cotton abandoned his support of those views only after he recognized they were endangering his ministry. Deputy Governor Dudley initially inverted the relationship between the two, perceiving Cotton as sharing *"Mrs. Hutchinson's judgment."* Certainly most Bay Colony ministers confused Hutchinson's views with Cotton's for some time, questioning him repeatedly in various meetings and conferences until he eventually managed to convince them that his views were orthodox. Shepard's letter was only the first of many subsequent inquiries concerning the soundness of Cotton's teachings on free grace and assurance.

Shepard's letter consisted of six queries, some with subpoints, which carried the unmistakable implication that Cotton had strayed into a reliance on inward spiritual impressions verging upon dangerous "Familistical" error. Chief among Shepard's concerns was whether Cotton advocated a reliance on inner impressions or "revelations" for assurance. This could open the door to a whole host of alarming ideas which Shepard and others like him traced back to the Familists and, behind them, to the chaos which had broken out at Munster. Reliance on inner impressions could cut a person entirely loose from the Bible and its moral constraints. It might lead men to forsake their spouses or multiply their wives by polygamy. It might lead an imbalanced man to conclude he was the Messiah. It might prompt this false messiah to amass a cadre of followers and attempt to seize control of Boston, bringing the whole New England enterprise to ruin in blood and fire.

Shepard therefore asked Cotton a series of applied questions designed to sniff out whether his colleague was sufficiently constrained by the text of the Bible. He wanted to know how Boston's teacher would counsel a Christian who detected evidence within herself that God had begun a saving work of grace as specified in a relevant passage of scripture. In one common conversion text, for example, God promised to "take away the stony heart out of your flesh" and "give you an heart of flesh" (Ezekiel 36:26). What if a young woman noticed new tenderness toward God in a heart which was once impervious to his grace? Should she use that passage as a diagnostic tool, interpreting her newfound tenderness as a sign that God had touched her own stony heart with his grace? Could she find in that experience a final resolution of her uncertainty about her salvation and "close with the Lord Jesus?" Or did she have to wait for a "more full, & clearer Revelation of the spirit?"

If the latter, Shepard wanted to know whether such a revelation was something more than the Spirit's personal illumination to the reader of the passage itself, "a thing beyond & above the word?" He did not think it "safe" to assert such an idea "because the spirit is not separated from the word but in it & is ever according to it." He warned Cotton that such expressions could easily be misconstrued by Familists who "honor word and ordinances" not so much as God's word but as places to "meet with the Spirit & their superlative raptures." For them, the Bible functioned only as a springboard into flights of purely subjective fancy.

Cotton rejected Shepard's invidious comparison of his own views with those of the Familists. If members of that sect used the Bible only as a gateway to frolic their own private "Revelations, & Raptures," Cotton wrote, they were clearly deluded. But he pled with Shepard not to equate "such a Delusion" to his own teaching concerning assurance. Cotton explained that while the Spirit's witness might reach "above and beyond the letter of the word" to provide "comfort & power to the soule"—an affirmation which made Shepard and other ministers nervous—yet it never became separated from Scripture as Familists believed. The Spirit never contradicted the Bible, but in fact bound a Christian's conscience to the Word. Thus, if the young woman mentioned above noticed her heart turning from stone to flesh as Ezekiel 36:26 said grace would do, she might well expect the Spirit to give her more. She could legitimately wait until she "got this Promise sealed" by a "further Anointment of the spirit," an inward sense of confidence that she was truly saved.

Events soon demonstrated that at the very least, Cotton and Shepherd—along with most other New England clergy—did not well "understand one another" over the issue of assurance. Or perhaps they understood one another too well. Shepard wanted to help his parishioners find assurance through close examination of all available evidence in their own hearts and experience. If they saw evidence of a divine promise of grace at work in their hearts, he wanted them to seize that opportunity to "close with Christ" immediately, accepting this as evidence that they were saved. If they engaged in a heartfelt observance of the means of grace, he wanted them to take courage from that practice of sanctification so long as they did not rely too much on their own righteousness. Cotton, by contrast, taught that any such effort to ground assurance on sanctification was at best inadequate and at worst might betray a person into relying on their own righteousness rather than Christ. The only safe basis for assurance lay in the direct, unconditional, and inward "Seal of the Spirit." For Shepard, this idea was neither necessary nor "safe." It could lead to despair if the inner witness never came and to Familist delusion if it did.

Shepard's circle remained unconvinced by Cotton's protest that his views on assurance had shaped his ministry for "many years both in old Boston, & in New." They found it anything but reassuring that a "diligent search" by Cotton among the members of his congregation had produced none, presumably including Anne Hutchinson herself, who "doe hold forth christ in any other way" than he himself did. For Shepard, the problem lay in the way Cotton himself "held forth Christ," even though the Boston teacher's conciliatory reply may have diffused confrontation for the moment.

John Cotton's reply to Shepard reveals the Boston teacher's impulse to minimize theological division and search for common ground, but the arrival of Anne Hutchinson's brother-in-law John Wheelwright in May brought a fighter for the "Free Grace" side of the controversy. Wheelwright had grown up in Lincolnshire near the Hutchinsons' home town of Alford. He had attended Sydney Sussex College, Cambridge with none other than Oliver Cromwell, who was reputed to have been "more afraid of meeting Wheelwright at football I have been since of meeting any army in the field, for I was infallibly sure of being tripped up by him." After earning his M.A. there, Wheelwright was ordained and soon became vicar of Bilsby near Alford. There he developed a reputation for preaching free grace in a manner consistent with Cotton's own views. He married William Hutchinson's youngest sister Mary shortly after his first wife died. William and Anne likely visited Bilsby many times to hear their brother-in-law preach. In 1632, however, Wheelwright was ejected from the Bilsby pulpit for simony—illegally selling his position as vicar back to the patron who had originally offered it to him. Whatever his reason for doing this, his family and many loyal parishioners understood his ouster as Laudian persecution. Cotton went into hiding the same year, and the coincidence certainly compounded Hutchinson's sense of trouble during that time "concerning the ministry under which I lived." It no doubt cheered her as her pregnancy and confinement neared their end to learn that the Wheelwrights had joined family and old Lincolnshire friends in Boston.

Wheelwright and his family found residence either in Boston or in Mount Wollaston, an area on the south shore of Massachusetts Bay which the General Court had recently added to Boston to provide more farmland for inhabitants. Wheelwright and Mary became members of the church at Boston on June 12, 1636. Throughout the following summer he participated in the exciting religious life of the town, expanding his circle of friends and attracting the attention of Governor Vane himself. Mary Wheelwright likely attended Anne Hutchinson's weekly meeting for women, and John probably led the mixed meeting at least occasionally. As a former minister himself, he also preached a guest sermon at least once and perhaps several times, either in Cotton's weekly lectures or on the Sabbath.

The theology Wheelwright advanced through informal conversations and occasional public preaching contrasted with the cautious introspection advocated by Thomas Shepard, probably even more sharply than Cotton's. The spiritual counsel he provided just three years earlier to one earnest inquirer, Hansard Knollys, would certainly have made Cotton uncomfortable because of its reliance on revelations and visions. Knollys recalled seeking Wheelwright's help during the early 1630s in determining whether he had received a "clear Call and Commission from Christ to preach." An interview convinced Wheelwright that his young inquirer had obtained a false sense of assurance "by performing duties, and rest[ing] in them." He sent Knollys away to pray, telling him to return in two or three days. At their next meeting the young man reported that he had received the witness of the Spirit from Hebrews 13:5, "I will never leave thee, nor forsake thee." Wheelwright told him he was "somewhat prepared to preach Jesus Christ and the Gospel of free grace to others, having been taught it of God, and having heard and learned it from Christ Jesus [him]self." Wheelwright told him to keep praying and God's Spirit soon spoke Acts 26:16 to his heart: "I have appeared unto thee for this purpose, to make thee a minister." God also gave Knollys a scripture text and doctrine in a dream, which Wheelwright confirmed as a direct divine commission to preach. Wheelwright continued to maintain throughout his life that the Holy Spirit was the "inward teacher" of every true Christian, giving both spiritual guidance and assurance of salvation by this sort of direct and absolute witness.

Anne Hutchinson embraced her brother-in-law John Wheelwright as a leader of the free grace faction of the godly in Boston alongside John Cotton, Governor Vane, and (though she may not have recognized it just yet) herself. Hutchinson, Vane, and Wheelwright would soon prove a volatile threesome. For the summer of 1636, however, they seemed primarily to have contented themselves with supporting Cotton's ministry, sustaining and enlarging the godly community through hospitality, acts of service, and spiritual activity. Thomas Weld, a longtime friend of Thomas Shepard, recalled in his preface to Winthrop's *Short Story* that Hutchinson and her circle would "labour to insinuate themselves into the affections" of other colonists. They would greet their neighbors warmly and cheerfully. They would behave politely and kindly toward their neighbors, giving them every consideration. They would invite others into their homes and would pay "friendly visits." Whenever newcomers arrived in Boston, Hutchinson and her friends "would be sure to welcome them." They would model Christian hospitality by showing newcomers "all courtesie." Hutchinson and her circle of friends would offer to put up newcomers "in their owne houses" until they could make other arrangements. Their religious observances also held great attraction for godly newcomers, giving Hutchinson and her friends the appearance of "very humble, holy, and spirituall Christians." They were models of self-sacrifice. They knew how to recite the Bible and use all the puritan buzz words. They could pray with "soule-ravishing expressions and affections." Newcomers who met these models of Christian goodness "could not but love and admire them."

Weld detected in Anne Hutchinson's activities a nefarious attempt to get newcomers "into their Web" so that they could "easily poyson them by degrees." Hutchinson herself, however, must have seen her hospitality and service as simple acts of Christian charity and social obligation. She did only what was commanded by the New Testament scriptures, and what was incumbent upon her as one of Boston's leading gentlewomen. Her friends, neighbors, and pastors certainly saw her in this light as well. John Cotton must have been especially gratified by the spirit of Christian cooperation and support Hutchinson's circle brought to the Boston congregation. It seems likely that throughout much of the summer of 1636, she continued to find what Cotton described as "loving and dear respect both from our Church-Elders and Brethren, and so from myself also among the rest."

By mid-October, however, a serious crack appeared in the unity of the Boston church, and John Winthrop fingered Anne Hutchinson as its source. The occasion was a campaign supported by Hutchinson and her friends to call John Wheelwright as a second teacher to the Boston church. The campaign originated in a petition by the residents of Mount Wollaston, an area about thirteen miles south along the Massachusetts shoreline which at that time belonged to Boston. Residents of "the Mount" (which later separated to become the town of Braintree) hoped that as

Boston's second teacher, Wheelwright could settle among them and provide regular preaching so they would not have to travel to Boston every week for worship.

Beyond this immediate issue, the controversy extended to include reports that Hutchinson had begun accusing many Bay Colony ministers of teaching a "covenant of works." Winthrop confined his own notes to two "dangerous errors" in Hutchinson's theology: "1. That the person of the Holy Ghost dwells in a justified person. 2. That no sanctification can help to evidence to us our justification." From these he detected the growth of another disturbing belief: since the indwelling Holy Ghost was the only sanctification available to a true Christian, good works constituted no more evidence of salvation for a true convert than for a hypocrite. Winthrop noted ominously that John Wheelwright "joined with [Mrs. Hutchinson] in these opinions."

The "secret quarrels" at which Thomas Shepard had hinted in the spring were beginning to "flame out" into the public conflagration of which he had warned Cotton, and Anne Hutchinson had emerged as their source. At the next meeting of the General Court on October 25, seven ministers—Thomas Shepard and his friends John Eliot and Thomas Weld, George Phillips, Hugh Peter, Richard Mather, and Nathaniel Ward—came from surrounding towns to "enter conference in private" with Hutchinson and her brother-in-law. Cotton's colleague John Wilson took notes during the meeting, and the ministers also called in for questioning Boston's lay elder Thomas Leverett and deacon John Coggeshall. The ministers hoped to "determine the certainty of" their views on assurance and grace. At the close of the conference, the ministers planned if necessary to write a letter of advice to the Boston congregation which could "prevent (if it were possible) the dangers which seemed hereby to hang over that and the rest of the churches." It would be Hutchinson's first official run-in with the colonial ministers, and the outcome would not bode well for her views.

Winthrop's own notes on this meeting remained focused on Wheelwright's views concerning the Holy Spirit. At Hutchinson's trial the next year, however, the ministers remembered a much broader discussion taking place that day. Winthrop noted that Cotton was also questioned at the meeting and "gave satisfaction" along with Wheelwright concerning their views on sanctification and the Holy Spirit. Hutchinson, however, did not. Cotton and Wheelwright agreed with their colleagues "that sanctification did help to evidence justification," though both continued to maintain that the inner witness of the Spirit provided the primary evidence of true conversion. The two admitted to teaching the doctrine Winthrop had identified as dangerous concerning the "indwelling of the person of the Holy Ghost." Yet they pointed out in conference that "some of the other ministers" also taught this doctrine and took care to distinguish it from "union with the person of the Holy Ghost," the view Winthrop attributed to "Mrs. Hutchinson and others."

This very fine but important distinction put Cotton and Wheelwright on the safe side of a controversy over what sort of a change took place in a person who experienced true conversion. Every puritan followed the Bible in believing that the convert became a "new creature." Mainstream puritans believed that the Spirit graciously provided a new set of holy desires and dispositions and empowered believers to act upon them. Winthrop and the sanctificationist ministers at the conference, however, thought that they detected something different in Hutchinson's views on the matter. To them what she said sounded too much like the dangerous, Familist-tinged notion that union with the Spirit somehow made the new creature either a third sort of being—part Holy Spirit and part human—or that the Spirit of Christ took up residence in the soul in such a way that his desires and dispositions overwhelmed those of the human spirit altogether. As such, their actions were no longer their own, but Christ's. Nothing the Christian did after such a union could be sin. From this it seemed only a short, logical step to the idea that a Christian could do absolutely anything he or she wanted; no deed was off limits.

Several ministers also recalled a confrontation with Hutchinson over their competence as pastors and teachers, though they differed over exactly what was said. According to the Salem minister Hugh Peter, Hutchinson declared that she detected "a wide and broad difference" between John Cotton's teaching and theirs, for "he preaches a covenant of grace and you a covenant of works." According to Peter, she added that they were "not able ministers of the new testament and know no more than the apostles did before the resurrection of Christ." Thomas Shepard recalled that she had told him he was not yet sealed with the Spirit. John Cotton, however, recalled that she had said, "he [Cotton] preaches the seal of the spirit upon free grace and you [Shepard and others] upon a work." Elder Thomas Leverett also insisted that she had stated only that "they did not preach a covenant of grace so clearly as Mr. Cotton did," explaining that they could not do so because like the Apostles they had not yet received the "witness of the spirit."

The conflicting statements of those present make it difficult to determine exactly what Hutchinson said, especially since they were made after memories had been corrupted by more than a year of acrimonious controversy. Winthrop's journal, the only record surviving from the period, states only that Hutchinson's doctrine of personal union with the Holy Spirit did not "satisfy" the visiting ministers as Cotton's and Wheelwright's clarification had done. Yet even the softer version of her statements as reported by Cotton and Leverett would have certainly antagonized ministers such as Shepard and Peter, men unaccustomed to being challenged by a layperson concerning their orthodoxy or spiritual condition. Peter probably remembered accurately that the ministers closed the meeting by charging the Boston elders to "speak further" with Hutchinson. Cotton promised that he would.

Hutchinson may have departed the meeting with the Bay Colony ministers under a cloud, but Wheelwright had reportedly assuaged their concerns. His supporters in the Boston church apparently believed that this conference cleared all suspicion concerning Wheelwright's orthodoxy, for five days later they went ahead with their plan to ordain him as the church's co-teacher. When they made the motion to call him, however, Winthrop stood up to oppose it on the grounds that the church was "well furnished already with able ministers, whose spirits they knew." He expressed concern that the hiring of Wheelwright might put the church's welfare in danger by "calling one whose spirit they knew not." He worried in particular about a sermon Wheelwright had earlier preached which included the suspect notion that "the person of the Holy Ghost and a believer were united." This was essentially the same issue which their fellow ministers had already resolved in both Wheelwright and Cotton's favor a few days earlier, and Governor Vane would not let Winthrop's charge pass unchallenged. After some discussion,

Winthrop conceded Wheelwright's orthodoxy, but continued to oppose him as an unruly spirit "apt to raise doubtful disputations." At this point, the church voted to release Wheelwright to accept a call to a new church "to be gathered at Mount Woollaston, now Braintree." His hope of becoming Cotton's colleague was dead. Winthrop had managed to block him from the Boston pulpit, but only at the cost of permitting residents of The Mount to establish their own separate church with Wheelwright as pastor.

Anne Hutchinson's brother-in-law had been blocked from ordination as a teacher of the Boston church, but only at the expense of the congregation's famous unity. Wheelwright's supporters naturally took offense, and the next day Winthrop tried to smooth over the differences. He confessed that he had wronged Wheelwright by "charging the brother in public" before confronting him privately, as the New England churches routinely required according to Jesus' instruction in Matthew 18. He also expressed regret that his "speech appeared in some bitterness" and hastened to assure the congregation that he "did love that brother's person and did honor the gifts and graces of God in him." Even so, Winthrop continued to justify his concern about Wheelwright's teaching on the Holy Spirit. He attributed the difficulty to "the brother's" use of "some words and phrases which were of human invention, and tended to doubtful disputation." Winthrop appealed to Wheelwright to express himself in simpler biblical terms, "seeing these variances grew (and with some estrangement withal)" from the expressions he had been using.

Winthrop's effort at reconciliation with Wheelwright's supporters offered too little and came too late. He had in fact sided with Shepard and other Bay Colony ministers against Anne Hutchinson's views on free grace. Neither side would retreat. Winthrop's stance not only set him in opposition to Hutchinson, her brother-in-law, and their supporters in the Boston church; it also contradicted the views of Governor Vane and, implicitly at least, their teacher John Cotton himself.

The battle lines had been drawn over free grace, assurance, and the role of the Holy Spirit in the believer's life. The divisions could no longer be covered with love. A time of trouble had come to the Bay Colony's churches and commonwealth. It would only subside with the exile of Anne Hutchinson.

5

Trouble in Churches and Commonwealth

John Winthrop sat in the governor's chair at the meeting of the General Court in Newtown at the opening of Anne Hutchinson's trial on November 7, 1637. Deputy Thomas Dudley sat to his right. The paper containing Hutchinson's indictment lay before him on the table. He fixed his gaze on the figure before him and began to speak. The Court knew that Mrs. Hutchinson had a "great share" in promoting "those opinions that are the causes of this trouble" in the colony, Winthrop declared. She was a close friend and ally of several whom the Court had sentenced to punishment only days earlier for the parts they had played in the recent disturbances. Even worse, she had made several statements which the Court regarded as "very prejudicial to the honour" of the colony's churches and ministers.

In the General Court's estimation, Hutchinson had incurred significant guilt by mere association with others who had taken part in political unrest during the past several months. It was enough for Winthrop that she had remained friends with members of what he saw as an antinomian faction after John Wheelwright's failed bid to become co-teacher of the Boston church. She had continued to entertain Wheelwright and his supporters in her home, despite the fact that he had preached a sermon the previous January which the General Court had branded seditious. In the Court's view, this made her as much a "transgressor of the law" as her guests.

As her prosecutors sought to depict matters, Hutchinson's guilt extended to action as well as association. She did not merely entertain Wheelwright's supporters in her home; she also held public meetings where she "disparaged all the ministers in the land." Furthermore, she exacerbated divisions in the Boston church by public displays of dissent staged whenever Pastor John Wilson officiated at the church's Sunday meetings. John Winthrop strove to characterize both her speech and her actions as political crimes, "greatly prejudicial to the state." He observed that the political unrest of 1637 had come only from those who attended her weekly meetings. She had undermined these colonists' deference to the colony's civil and religious leaders. Instead, the partisans of free grace had begun taking their cues from her. Winthrop depicted Hutchinson's meetings as the nucleus of a rival political faction in Massachusetts Bay, one which advanced its bid for power through promoting the doctrine of free grace.

Winthrop's strenuous effort to depict Anne Hutchinson's actions in political terms reveals how much of a threat the free grace faction had become to the leaders of church and state in Massachusetts Bay. Embedded in the indictment against Hutchinson was the implication that she had compounded her errors by transgressing a customary line which confined women to the private society of home and informal relations within the community. Yet Hutchinson persistently denied this claim. She viewed her actions as the legitimate efforts of a well-to-do merchant's wife and a gentlewoman in her own right. She enjoyed a respect and social standing which in this New World setting could rival the claims of families only a few rungs higher on the social ladder—families such as the Winthrops and the Dudleys.

As we have seen, Anne Hutchinson had extended her influence by pursuing activities widely recognized as proper to women. As a woman skilled in healing and midwifery, she had earned the affection, gratitude, and support of many families in Boston. Her skill had made her a "profitable member" among the colonists during much of her first two years there, as Winthrop himself acknowledged. Even the meetings she hosted were widely regarded as legitimate women's activity, a point which Winthrop was eventually forced to concede at her trial. Yet the

"Flewentness of her Tongue," coupled with her "ready wit and bold spirit," combined after October of 1636 to make her a steadily growing threat to the political stability of the Massachusetts Bay. Her status as a gentlewoman and her support within a large, private community of Boston women—which lay by its very definition outside the public political community of men—only increased the potency of that threat.

Even so, the General Court had not indicted Hutchinson alone. They had included her among a cluster of several ringleaders in a faction whose activities seemed increasingly dangerous. The danger lay in the concerted activities of several strong personalities, not one individual. It is impossible to understand the Court's actions against Anne Hutchinson without reconstructing the combined activities of all of these leaders. The males in the group—men such as John Cotton, John Wheelwright, and Sir Henry Vane—usually occupied the foreground events of 1636–1637. By contrast, Hutchinson usually acted within the private spaces of colonial life. Most of her deeds during this period occurred out of view of the public record and thus remain frustratingly invisible to historians.

It is also impossible to understand the heated response of Bay Colony officials apart from the convergence of three significant external threats in 1636–1637. The internal divisions of the free grace controversy could not have come at a worse time. The first threat came from the French colony to the north. French traders had for some time been competing with the colonists for a toehold in the fur trade with the Abenakis in what is now Maine. In 1633, a party of French under the command of Acadian governor Charles la Tour had captured a small trading post, set up at Penobscot by men from Plymouth, killing two of the English in the process. La Tour's action constituted a reassertion of earlier French claims to this territory and its trade, which threatened to block both Massachusetts and Plymouth from important sources of fur. In December 1636, Governor Vane received a letter from another French commander, Charles d'Aulnay, which seemed to hint that the French would soon invade Massachusetts and Plymouth.

The outbreak of hostilities between English colonists and the Pequot Indians posed a second grave danger to Massachusetts Bay. Many colonists interpreted the Pequot War as a demonic threat from without which mirrored the devilish "Familistical" dissent within. Open hostility broke out in September of 1636 after two years of tension caused by the influx of English settlement along the Connecticut and Mystic rivers. That fall, an expeditionary force from Massachusetts Bay burned Pequot homes and crops on Block Island, to the south of Narragansett Bay. Pequot warriors retaliated by besieging Fort Saybrook, near the mouth of the Connecticut River. Throughout the winter and spring of 1636–1637, they carried on a campaign of raiding English settlements and harassing overland travelers.

Pequot leaders viewed these desperate acts as justifiable retaliation for the English depredations on Block Island, but the colonists detected in them the work of Satan himself. Massachusetts military captain John Underhill labeled the Pequots "wicked imps" who imitated "the devil, their commander" by running "up and down as roaring lions, compassing all corners of the country for their prey, seeking whom they might devour." Meanwhile, colonists on each side of the free grace controversy suspected the devil was in their own midst as well, stirring dissension through the speech and actions of those on the opposing side. A state of war with native adversaries demanded colonial unity, not the "disturbances, divisions, and contentions" which had overtaken Massachusetts Bay at this critical time.

If threats from the French and the Pequots were not enough, Bay Colony leaders were further unsettled by fresh rumors from England that the Crown was preparing to revoke their charter and install a new government over the entire region. For the past several years, agents of the Massachusetts Bay had been fending off efforts by powerful rivals to challenge their charter and strengthen royal control of the Bay Colony. In 1633, William Laud took control of a newly created Commission for Regulating Plantations and launched an investigation into the affairs and actions of the Massachusetts Bay Company. In 1635, the King's Privy Council turned up the heat by initiating a lawsuit in the Court of King's Bench to repeal the company charter. The case was nearing conclusion during the winter of 1636–1637, just as the conflict over free grace was heating up in Massachusetts.

Under these circumstances, any reports back to England of the controversy surrounding Anne Hutchinson and her circle of friends could prove fatal to the puritan experiment. Laud had founded his English campaign against the puritans by lumping sanctificationists such as Shepard with the most radical preachers of the 1620s and 1630s, arguing that puritan ideas were inherently Antinomian and Familistical. Damaging news about Roger Williams's radical views had already reached London. Word of fresh strife in the Bay Colony over free grace views could hand Laud's commission an ideal pretext for installing a harsh new regime to enforce conformity to the Church of England.

Colonial leaders remained acutely aware of the combined threat represented by the French, the Pequot, and the machinations back in England. Both sanctificationists and Anne Hutchinson's allies saw these threats as looming instruments of God's providential discipline for the sin of strife among the churches of Massachusetts Bay. In December of 1636, Governor Vane, Hutchinson's most powerful ally, professed to detect in them "the inevitable danger . . . of God's judgments to come upon us for these differences and dissensions." The New England minister Thomas Weld spoke for the opposing sanctificationists when he too termed the controversy a "new storme" sent by God to test the colonists. Indeed, the growing controversy so concerned the deputies of the Massachusetts General Court that they called for a general fast "to be held in all the churches" on January 20, 1637. The reasons included "the dangers of those at Connecticut, and of ourselves also, by the Indians; and the dissensions in our churches."

By the time this fast was called, the dissension over how to gain assurance of salvation was nearing the boiling point. To the colonists this was not the arcane religious dispute it seems today. It was desperately urgent. The very souls of the disputants hung in the balance. Leaders like Anne Hutchinson and John Wheelwright believed that a truly Reformed church should include a commitment to free grace. They saw sanctificationists as slipping dangerously close to a kind of "works righteousness" as pernicious in its own way as that of Archbishop Laud. It could deceive those who followed it into basing their salvation on their own good deeds and so send them straight to Hell. Sanctificationists such as Thomas Shepard and John Winthrop, by contrast, thought that free gracers were trying to highjack their godly commonwealth, turning it into a place of anarchy and licentiousness.

The sanctificationists' fears had prompted Winthrop to speak against Wheelwright's ordination to the Boston church the previous October. The controversy this sparked had only grown in ensuing months. Boston's church leaders—Pastor John Wilson, Teacher John Cotton, and prominent laymen including ruling elder Thomas Leverett, Sir Henry Vane, and John Winthrop—had attempted to manage internal differences quietly. In November, for example, they conducted a "disputation" over Vane's contention that the Holy Ghost formed a "personal union" with true believers—a sort of fusion of personalities which some understood to swallow up the will and actions of a believer into those of God himself. To Winthrop and Wilson, Vane's notion sounded uncomfortably close to some radical ideas which English puritans had joined Laudians in condemning, but they were well aware that many church members sympathized with him. Consequently, they sought to keep tempers from flaring by confining the dispute to writing. The leaders concluded it weakly with a resolution to avoid applying the term "person" to the Holy Spirit because it seemed to produce more confusion than clarity.

The other Bay Colony ministers, most of whom were sanctificationists, also got into the act by calling a conference in December to draw up a list of sixteen questions in which they suspected that John Cotton differed from them. They pressed him to provide a direct answer for each. Cotton promised to respond, also in writing, in the hope of achieving resolution and restoring unity among the churches.

Neither effort could keep the conflict completely out of the public eye, nor could it keep colonists from talking about it in their homes, over their back fences, or when they met in the street. In fact, the most significant center of the strife was Anne Hutchinson's parlor, a place outside the formal public realm of minister and magistrate. Hutchinson's private, semi-weekly meetings served to rally the supporters of Vane, Wheelwright, and Cotton and to keep the debate bubbling among the rank and file of the Boston church. By this time, the controversy was certainly helping to attract a full complement of between sixty and eighty people who tramped through the December mud and snow to the Hutchinsons' door. Even though Anne and William had built one of the largest houses in town, with a parlor most likely sized to match, numbers this large would have filled every corner and may sometimes have spilled out the doors. As we have seen, Hutchinson conducted the women's meetings herself in a question-and-answer format, leaving the mixed meetings to the leadership of unnamed men, who almost certainly included Wheelwright on occasion.

Discussion at Hutchinson's meetings continued to revolve around her belief that only the direct witness of the Spirit could assure true believers that they were God's elect. Related questions ranged into such arcane matters as whether true conversion completely replaced a believer's personality and will with that of the Holy Spirit, and whether the Spirit could speak to the soul apart from the Bible (John Winthrop eventually collected a list of eighty-two "erroneous opinions" allegedly advanced at one or another of Hutchinson's meetings). They also included the belief among at least some of Hutchinson's followers that one had received this witness or "seale of the Spirit" could detect infallibly whether another person who claimed to be saved was truly elect or a mere imposter. Hutchinson's conference with Shepard and others the previous October suggests that she had been making such judgments since the summer of 1636. After Wheelwright's failed bid for a Boston pastorate, her judgments apparently became less guarded. She almost certainly began to question Pastor John Wilson's fitness for his office and likely also began labeling John Winthrop a hypocrite.

While Hutchinson continued to host private discussions in her home, the struggle over free grace also heated up within the exclusively male preserve of politics. Since Hutchinson conducted her meetings and pursued her activities outside the public arena, they remained officially unnoticed for several months. She appears virtually nowhere in the surviving records from the winter, spring, and summer of 1637, which document exclusively the controversy among the ministers and magistrates. Yet the actions of the colony's political leadership remained intimately bound up with Hutchinson's actions in the private, informal life of the colonial community. Her own eventual trials cannot be understood apart from the public actions taken during these months by men such as Governor Henry Vane and her brother-in-law John Wheelwright.

During its meeting of December 1636, the General Court signaled official concern over the free grace controversy by asking the colony's ministers for advice about identifying and pacifying the differences among the colony's churches. At one point in the discussion, the sanctificationist Hugh Peter of Salem declared to Governor Vane that there had been no conflict among the churches before Vane had come to Massachusetts. Vane retorted that controversy had only come because he brought the truth with him, for "the light of the gospel brings a sword." The young governor also drew on a well-known passage in the New Testament book of Galatians to declare that "the children of the bondwoman"—those who clung to a Covenant of Works—would "persecute the freewoman"—those who shared Vane's own views concerning the Covenant of Grace. Pastor John Wilson also opened a public breach at this session between himself and John Cotton when he blamed the controversies in Boston and other towns upon the "new opinions risen up amongst us."

These events of the General Court's December session served to ratchet up the tension even further. In its aftermath, Cotton and other members confronted Wilson privately over the public statement he had made about the disruptive impact of "new opinions" concerning free grace which Vane, Hutchinson, Wheelwright, and even Cotton had been advancing. When Wilson refused to acknowledge any fault for criticizing free grace views before the General Court, the Boston congregation issued a formal call for him to "answer publicly" in an open meeting. There order broke down completely as Vane remonstrated heatedly against Wilson for what he had said to the General Court. Nearly everyone except Winthrop and one or two others joined in the attack on Wilson, many "with much bitterness and reproaches." Cotton, though siding with the majority, did his best to turn down the heat. He refused to allow a formal congregational vote of censure against Wilson, but did give his colleague a "grave exhortation" which Winthrop described as filled with "much wisdom and moderation." The next day Wilson preached the sermon and Vane, in an effort to paper over the breach, made a public statement praising its contents. Even so, the controversy of the day before revealed that Boston's pastor had lost the support of nearly the entire Boston congregation.

On the eve of the fast day, the frigid January air was crackling with tension. A public breach had opened between the pastor and teacher of Massachusetts Bay's flagship congregation, revealing a larger fault line dividing the colony's ministry. Indeed, the regulars at Anne Hutchinson's meetings had become convinced that apart from John Cotton and John Wheelwright, the clergy were preaching dangerously close to a covenant of works. In Hutchinson's view, this placed the very souls of the colonists in peril. Persons who sat under what she termed the "legal preaching" of such ministers might be misled into trusting their good works to save them, thus remaining bound for hell "under a covenant of works." Visitors to Boston carried home reports of what was being said at the Hutchinson house. Others from outlying communities who had attended lectures by Cotton or Wheelwright went home lamenting that their own ministers did not preach the covenant of grace so clearly. Such sentiments began to engender pockets of discontent and strain within other churches of the bay. Colonial leaders desperately hoped that a day of communal fasting and preaching would help to calm the situation. Instead, John Wheelwright's Fast Day Sermon in Boston drove tensions even higher. The choice of Wheelwright to preach that day suggests that the influence of Hutchinson's circle in the Boston church had reached its peak. The Hutchinson circle was determined to use their influence to defend free grace, not to temporize with proponents of a covenant of works.

Wheelwright's sermon did not disappoint his sister-in-law and her circle of supporters. He opened by declaring that this fast was necessary since the ministers had provoked the Lord to depart by making the colonists groan under the burden of the Covenant of Works. He proposed a twofold remedy. First, Wheelwright urged his listeners to guard against Christ being "taken from us" by any minister or magistrate who attempted to stifle the doctrine of free grace. Second, he encouraged the audience to prepare for spiritual combat against any who attempted to impose the Covenant of Works through their preaching. Wheelwright argued that such persons betrayed themselves any time they encouraged a convert to find assurance of salvation in a work of sanctification, even one so praiseworthy as hungering and thirsting for God or loving a neighbor.

True assurance, Wheelwright declared, came only from a direct spiritual encounter with Christ through an inner witness of the Spirit. Those who promoted any other means of assurance had more in common with Roman Catholic "Papists" than with godly Protestants. Indeed, they exposed themselves as Antichristian enemies to the Lord. If opposition to sanctificationist doctrine caused a "combustion in the Church and commonwealth," that was only to be expected. After all, Jesus himself had "come to send fire upon the earth," and the Holy Spirit desired to set that fire alight by promoting free grace. It should be the desire of all true saints as well.

In declaring sanctificationists "Antichristian," Wheelwright had publicly expressed a key idea in Anne Hutchinson's own theology. At her trial the following November, she too described a time when she had come to realize that those who did not teach the new covenant possessed "the spirit of antichrist." From that day, she told the court, the Lord had "let me see which was the clear ministry and which the wrong." Drawing on a common allegorical interpretation of the Old Testament Song of Solomon, she explained that she had learned "to distinguish between the voice of my beloved"—Christ speaking assurance to her own soul—and "Moses"—the antichristian message of "legal obedience" found in the Covenant of Works. She also knew how to distinguish among preachers. Some—Cotton and Wheelwright, for example—preached the in the voice of Christ. Others—Thomas Shepard perhaps—were "John the Baptists," who had not yet received the Spirit and therefore preached a Covenant of Grace less clearly. Unnamed others were "antichrists"—John the Baptists gone bad, who persisted in preaching without the Spirit's witness, and as a result actively directed people away from Christ to the bondage and spiritual death inherent in the Covenant of Works.

This belief apparently formed another important thread in Hutchinson's weekly teachings at the meetings in her house. She sought not only to help others receive assurance through the witness of the Spirit, but also to hone their own ability to distinguish those who preached with the voice of Christ and those who countered in the tones of antichrist. Some of her followers learned the lesson all too well, as a much later recollection by the immigrant Edward Johnson suggests. Johnson recalled encountering a follower of Hutchinson's sometime after arriving in Boston in 1636. "Come along," the man said, "i'le bring you to a Woman that Preaches better Gospell then any of your black-coates that have been at the Ninneversity." Since the university only made ninnies of the colonial ministers, Hutchinson's follower preferred to learn from a woman who "speaks through the meere motion of the spirit, without any study at all."

Wheelwright's Fast Day Sermon effectively constituted a declaration of spiritual war on every colonial black-coated ninny except himself and Cotton, the only two who did not encourage converts to find assurance in works of sanctification. Indeed, the fiery preacher had at one point in his sermon invoked apocalyptic imagery which compared the controversy to the great final battle between the hosts of heaven and hell. He predicted that the gospel of free grace would subject the "Whore of Babylon" to a spiritual burning. The divine fire would destroy not only Rome and the papal Antichrist there, but the purveyors of the covenant of works in New England as well. Who knew, Wheelwright suggested, but that the Jews would be converted and the New Jerusalem ushered in? Such words sounded frighteningly similar to the kind of preaching which had sparked the revolt at Muenster a hundred years before.

In the aftermath of Wheelwright's sermon, John Winthrop noted in his diary that the "the differences in the said points of religion increased more and more . . . so as all men's mouths were full of them." Anne Hutchinson and other members of the Boston church continued the practice of attending weekday lectures by many neighboring ministers. Yet when the sermon ended and the minister opened the floor for questions, he frequently faced a barrage of hostile queries and objections which one of the targets, Thomas Weld, compared to "half a dozen

Pistols discharged in the face of the Preacher." To be fair, Weld and other preachers who received such treatment had often provoked it by denouncing free grace views from the pulpit.

In the Boston church itself, Anne Hutchinson and several of her female followers began to exit the meetinghouse whenever Pastor Wilson began his part of Sunday worship. Rev. Thomas Weld recalled that they made a spectacle of "rising up, and contemptuously turning their backs upon the faithfull Pastor . . . when he began to pray or preach." John Cotton later recalled that the women offered him personal reasons for walking out—reasons related to women's health or hygiene—which he found difficult or perhaps too delicate to challenge.

Hutchinson's acts of protest against Wilson's ministry offer a glimpse into her specifically feminine tactics of leadership during this period. All sides recognized her role as one of the field marshals in the spiritual war for free grace. Yet no one ever pinned on her any direct violation of gender norms in advocating her point of view. She executed her command within the formal boundaries of a seventeenth-century gentlewoman's social sphere. Hutchinson maintained the loyalty and respect of Boston's women by carrying on as she had since her arrival. She continued to assist women in childbirth. She kept tending to the sick of the community. She went on extending hospitality to newcomers. As one of Boston's leading women, she continued teaching the community's women in a weekly meeting whose size and regularity may have raised eyebrows, but which nevertheless fell squarely within the biblical mandate that older women should instruct the younger.

Hutchinson very effectively deployed her followers through a feminine network which she forged through the use of her natural intelligence, gentry status, and selfless service. Together they battled for free grace in a manner similar to many other effective seventeenth-century English women, who exercised great influence in the affairs of Church and State through informal channels of female friendship and obligation. Hutchinson numbered among her friends and supporters the wives of several leading men of Boston. She may even have won the friendship of Pastor Wilson's wife Elizabeth, who once took the unusual step of joining him in a private conference with some of Hutchinson's supporters.

Hutchinson's detractors noticed this pattern, charging that she and her circle commonly worked first upon women, hoping "by them, as by an Eve, to catch their husbands also."

Hutchinson may seldom have intended much more than to extend charity and hospitality to her Christian sisters, yet her actions amassed influence which she could draw upon when the time came to defend her view of assurance. Her female friends could persuade their husbands to support public advocates of free grace such as Cotton and Wheelwright and to exercise their own public roles by voting in congregational meetings for leaders and policies which would support free grace as well as voting for representatives to the General Court who sympathized with their views. They could bring their husbands to the Hutchinsons' weekly mixed meeting to woo them to the doctrines of free grace. Women could also register their own displeasure with "legall" praying or preaching in weekly meetings and lectures by invoking unspecified female excuses to walk out.

Historians have offered a variety of explanations for why Anne Hutchinson and her followers advocated so strenuously for the doctrines of free grace. Some have argued that her ideas concerning assurance held significant implications for greater personal autonomy and equality and that these implications led Hutchinson herself to act in supposedly "unfeminine" ways. Yet there is no evidence that Anne Hutchinson ever intended to launch any overt challenge to seventeenth century gender roles, and none of her allies ever perceived such an agenda in their own views. Others have argued that the doctrines of free grace were more individualistic and therefore more congenial to core merchant families of Boston such as the Hutchinsons, who opposed efforts by the colonial majority to limit profits and harness trade to traditional communal ends. Yet under scrutiny this division also breaks down, since even farmers in the Massachusetts countryside participated in the rampant price gouging of the 1630s, and merchants such as William Hutchinson cooperated in efforts to bring such profiteering under the community's control.

It seems best to take seriously the express reasons offered by members of Hutchinson's and her circle for their passionate advocacy of free grace. John Wheelwright had argued in his Fast

Day Sermon that the true Gospel—the way of salvation itself—was at stake and with it the souls of the colonists and the very purpose of their coming to Massachusetts Bay. If the assurance of justification came by faith as a work, he declared, "it is not Gospell." Any who advocated such views were no better than followers of the Pope, whom the puritans regarded the very embodiment of Antichrist. Ever since Wheelwright's incendiary sermon, Winthrop noted in his diary, it had become "as common here to distinguish between men, by being under a covenant of grace or a covenant of works, as in other countries between Protestants and Papists." The free grace Controversy had become the puritan commonwealth's equivalent of the seventeenth-century European wars of religion, with each side vying for the reigns of political power so that it could secure the truth of the Gospel.

The March meeting of the General Court revealed that the colony's political winds were blowing strongly against Hutchinson's circle and the Boston church as a whole. To be sure, the free grace views of Hutchinson and her allies had found a scattered following outside of Boston, but most colonists remained unconvinced by them. Indeed, most were puzzled and offended by the idea that their faithful pastors, whom they had braved the hazards of ocean travel to join in Massachusetts, were preaching the works righteousness of Rome. They had received comfort from the ministers' preaching and found assurance from their counsel. They had tested their pastors' words against their own reading of scripture and found the two consistent. This balance in favor of the sanctificationists was reflected in the discussions of the Court itself. To be sure, Winthrop observed that any mention of free grace views produced a division, "yet the greater number far were sound." Most shared the sanctificationist view that good works of sanctification provided reliable evidence of true salvation. The majority moved quickly against free grace opinions, censuring "one Stephen Greensmith" and fining him the huge sum of £40 (well beyond a year's wages) for saying that all the ministers "except A. B. C." taught a covenant of works.

The court next tried John Wheelwright for criticizing in his Fast Day Sermon those who taught that sanctification could evidence true salvation and for "stirring up the people" with bitter, inflammatory rhetoric. Wheelwright protested that he had directed his words only toward those who made a practice of examining their good works and inner dispositions for evidence of true faith. At this, several astute members of the court turned to some sanctificationist ministers who were present and asked whether they observed such a practice. The ministers solemnly acknowledged that they did. Their reply provided all the evidence the court needed to convict Wheelwright of sedition—a very serious offence. The court added a conviction of contempt for good measure, since it had initially appointed the fast to assist in reconciling the differences over free grace. Wheelwright had deliberately done just the opposite—he had thrown more fuel on the fire.

The outcome of John Wheelwright's trial was enormously unpopular in Boston. This made the town an uncomfortable location for the majority of deputies—most of whom came from the surrounding communities—who voted to convict him. Governor Vane and a few supporters tendered a formal protest against the conviction. The court rejected it. The church of Boston also submitted an extremely angry petition defending Wheelwright. The Court chose to avoid fanning the flames any further and left the petition unanswered. It also voted to delay sentencing until its May session, and to move the May session to Newtown. The move would carry the session away from the Boston townspeople whose contention had dogged the March proceedings. Indeed, the location of the May Court in Thomas Shepard's meetinghouse helped to shift the balance of influence to the sanctificationists.

The stage was set for the General Court's majority to make a strong bid for the governor's office at the annual election in May. In the meantime, however, the heat of contention continued. Thomas Shepard stepped up his efforts to counter the "Familistical" influences he perceived in Boston through preaching his extended sermon cycle on Jesus' parable of the ten virgins (Matthew 25:1–13). Anne Hutchinson's supporters in the Boston church became increasingly alienated from other puritans in the Bay Colony as the verbal attacks on "legal preaching" persisted. Even John Cotton got into the act, remaining conspicuously absent from the organizational meeting of a new church at Concord, as did Governor Vane, John Wheelwright, and the two ruling elders of the Boston church. The reason for their absence, John Winthrop noted in his diary, was thought to be that Cotton and the others considered Concord's chosen ministers, Peter Bulkeley and John Jones, "legal preachers" and would not endorse their ordination.

Such behavior must have distressed the ordinarily accommodating Cotton, who was finding it increasingly difficult to steer a course between the two sides. Although his own sympathies lay with Anne Hutchinson's circle, he was receiving increasing pressure to close ranks with the sanctificationists against her ideas on free grace and assurance. Shortly before the March meeting of the General Court, he had preached a farewell sermon urging a group of passengers bound for England to minimize any rumors of dissent which had been filtering back home, toward the cocked ears of Archbishop Laud. He suggested they offer the ambiguous explanation that the dispute was about "magnifying the grace of God." One side—he did not specify which—wanted to "advance the grace of God within us," while the other sought to "advance the grace of God towards us." Cotton's colleague John Wilson followed up with a sermon insisting that he knew of no minister in the colony who did not "labor to advance the free grace of God in justification." He went on to argue that the search for assurance in sanctification did not contradict free grace, a statement at which some of Hutchinson's circle took offense. Nevertheless, John Winthrop observed that colonists who had not followed the intricacies of the controversy could scarcely distinguish between Cotton's and Wilson's views. There was ample room for accommodation, and Cotton's fellow ministers labored to negotiate with him a united position on assurance and sanctification. They also labored to reconcile Cotton and Wilson.

In the months before the crucial May meeting of the General Court, the male leaders of Hutchinson's circle were preparing for a political showdown. While Hutchinson continued her weekly meetings outside the official public arena, several of Boston's leading men organized a petition requesting the General Court to reconsider its censure of John Wheelwright. Organizers argued that Wheelwright did not preach his Fast Day

Sermon in contempt of the General Court but from a heartfelt desire to fulfill the court's purpose by inspiring in his listeners more devotion for Christ. Nor was his sermon seditious, as the court had charged. The petitioners urged the Court to consider the possibility that its own members had inadvertently enacted the will of Satan by convicting Wheelwright. After all, the Devil habitually sought to slander God's faithful preachers, often acting through just such misguided actions such as the General Court's conviction of their champion. The petitioners suggested that if the court did not reverse itself and acquit Wheelwright, God would explode in wrath against those who dared to "meddle against the Prophets of God."

May 17 dawned bright and clear. Most members of the General Court had traveled to Newtown the night before, though some from nearby towns traveled by boat or on foot that morning to reach the Newtown town common by 1:00 p.m. The Boston delegation had brought along a petition signed by seventy-four supporters of John Wheelwright. The tension mounted as Governor Vane arrived with his armed, four-man honor guard to call the Court to order. Immediately the Boston delegation stepped forward to present their *Remonstrance or Petition*. Before Vane could begin a public reading, however, Deputy Governor Winthrop objected that the petition was out of order. This was a court for elections, he declared. According to precedent, a new governor and his assistants must be chosen before petitions could be heard. Vane balked, sparking debate over the order of business which threatened to run all day. Winthrop eventually broke the deadlock by calling for a vote over procedure. The majority voted for election and began making their way toward one corner of the common, where John Wilson had climbed an oak tree and was urging the freeholders to vote. Vane and his Boston supporters remained where they were until Winthrop declared that the court would simply proceed to election without him. Vane bowed to reality and stepped forth to order the election. The vote went decisively to Winthrop for Governor and Thomas Dudley for Deputy. Sir Henry Vane, along with two elected assistants who were Hutchinson supporters, William Coddington and Richard Dummer, found themselves "left quite out" of government.

The free grace faction did not take defeat gracefully, and their bitter display of indignation served to confirm the impression that its advocates were dangerous troublemakers. John Winthrop, whom the great majority of the General Court had returned to the governorship to replace Vane, recorded that "there was a great danger of tumult that day." The record does not indicate whether Anne Hutchinson herself was present, though she, like other colonial women, may have gone to Newtown to observe the proceedings. Many of her male allies were there to support Vane, however, and several of them burst into "fierce speeches" as others began to shove and wrestle. Yet they soon recognized they were in the minority and lapsed into sullen silence. The four men in Vane's honor guard laid down their halberds (combination spears and battle axes) and went home, deliberately snubbing the new governor. To save some face, Winthrop recruited two of his own servants as substitutes for a position usually filled by sergeants from the local military company.

Such displays did not prevent the General Court's majority from attempting to quell the dispute over free grace by political means in the days that followed. The Court's effort received a boost when John Cotton released a statement reducing his differences with other ministers to "a very narrow scantling," and Thomas Shepard preached an Election Day Sermon which "brought them yet nearer," in John Winthrop's view. The combined effect, observed Winthrop, made the differences appear so small that, if the parties had not already become so polarized, they might easily have reconciled. Winthrop was no doubt exaggerating, given the high level of tension which persisted throughout the summer. Nevertheless, the sanctificationists within the General Court clearly held the upper hand. The Court haled in Hutchinson's "brother Wheelwright" and ordered him to consider carefully that if he would only retract and correct his error, the court might go easy on him. If he continued to refuse, however, he could expect no mercy. Wheelwright remained defiant. He refused to retract his statements and promised to appeal if the Court sentenced him. Even so, the Court postponed his sentence to the next session.

The General Court could now afford this display of magnanimity. The election had demonstrated that the majority possessed "power enough to have crushed" Anne Hutchinson, her brother-in-law, and their allies. Yet it had exercised restraint in the very face of the free grace faction's unruly behavior and provocative speeches. Postponement of Wheelwright's sentence could only make the majority's moderation and desire for reconciliation evident to any colonist with an open mind.

As Hutchinson and her associates saw matters, however, the election's winners were antichrists, proponents of a false gospel that threatened to kill souls. In the ensuing months, Sir Henry Vane and John Wheelwright spurned gestures of reconciliation. Hutchinson herself continued to criticize the sanctificationist ministers in her weekly meetings and to walk out of the meetinghouse whenever a sanctificationist minister officiated. Vane and William Coddington, who had customarily shared seats of honor with John Winthrop in church, ostentatiously stood up and walked across the meeting house to the deacon's seat on the Sunday after the election. Vane refused Winthrop's invitation to return, and thereafter snubbed him whenever the two met in public settings.

While Hutchinson continued to advocate her views of free grace in her private weekly meetings, her allies also carried on a campaign of protest against their rivals. They continued to pepper ministers with hostile questions on lecture days. The women of Hutchinson's circle kept making unspecified excuses to stand up and walk out of a meeting conducted by a minister whom they opposed. When the General Court chose Boston pastor John Wilson as chaplain to the colony's expedition against the Pequots, the men of the town's free grace faction expressed public disapproval of Wilson's chaplaincy by refusing to join the expedition. The town sent only one or two who were out of favor because they supported Wilson along with a few others widely regarded as ne'er-do-wells. Hutchinson and her allies refused even to offer a civil farewell to their pastor. By this time, the townspeople's defiance did not represent a serious security threat. The Pequot stronghold at Mystic had fallen to the colonists, and the war had shifted to mopping up a few pockets of resistance. Nevertheless, this behavior gave conspicuous expression to the free grace faction's judgment that Wilson and the governor who commissioned him were "enemies, Antichrists, and persecutors" of all who defended free grace.

The free grace faction's persistent behavior shows how the sting of defeat in May's elections still lingered in spite of the General Court's restraint towards Wheelwright. In one respect the new Court had further exacerbated tensions by forbidding any newcomer from remaining more than three weeks in any town without official permission. The Court had taken this action specifically to prevent the immigration of any new colonists who might share the opinions of Anne Hutchinson and John Wheelwright. In July, John Winthrop sparked a fresh round of contention when he enforced this order against Hutchinson's newly arrived brother-in-law, Samuel Hutchinson, along with some of Wheelwright's friends. His decision provoked bitter protests in the Boston church and a sharp response from Sir Henry Vane, who charged that Winthrop had arbitrarily denied the newcomers permission to settle out of mere prejudice rather than a genuine concern for the common good.

Vane's principled challenge to Winthrop's action proved to be a parting shot. Within a few short weeks, Anne Hutchinson, her extended family, and their friends found themselves standing on the Boston wharf waving goodbye to their champion Sir Henry Vane. The young firebrand had decided to return to England, ostensibly to take care of pressing family matters. His supporters hoped the absence would be only temporary. He had lost the governorship and political influence, but Hutchinson shared with others the hope that Vane would draw on connections in England to set matters right. Indeed, Vane's influence at home had made it far too risky for Winthrop and the General Court to act directly against him or other members of the free grace faction while their noble champion remained in the colony. By August 3, however, this "chief supporter" was out of the picture, at least temporarily.

John Cotton had also considered leading an emigration from the colony to defuse the controversy, but Winthrop and his fellow ministers had persuaded him to stay. As Vane sailed off, Cotton was on the verge of coming to terms with the colony's ministers. The free grace faction's influence was dwindling.

Even so, the Winthrop and the majority in the General Court still considered Hutchinson and her circle dangerous—perhaps the most immediate danger the colony now faced. The Pequots had been defeated in the spring of 1637. Captive survivors had been marched through the streets of Boston and sold as slaves to colonial buyers. For the time being, the risk of French invasion, which was always greater in the colonists' imagination than in reality, had faded into the background. The Court of King's Bench had demanded surrender of the charter, but unrest at home had distracted the Crown's attention from colonial affairs. The General Court's authority remained intact. The May election had placed that authority firmly into the hands of those who supported the sanctificationists. It had become clear that nearly every New England minister other than Cotton and Wheelwright held sanctificationist views. The Court could begin moving deliberately to isolate and bring down Hutchinson and Wheelwright. The end game in the free grace controversy was about to begin.

Trial

Anne Hutchinson scanned the interior of the Newtown meeting house as she entered in answer to the General Court's summons. The deputies of the colony towns flanked the governor and his deputy on either side, confronting her with a wall of hostile faces. She drew sympathetic glances from Boston's two deputies to the Court, William Coddington and William Colburn, but she could take only little hope from their presence. John Cotton sat among a cluster of black-coated ministers which included three of her most determined opponents—Thomas Shepard, Hugh Peter, and Thomas Weld. Despite Cotton's recent reconciliation with these men, Anne remained confident that his testimony would favor her when the right moment came. She also recognized Thomas Leverett, an elder in the Boston Church who had always supported Cotton and might at least testify without prejudice. Her neighbor and family friend John Coggeshall was on hand to offer what help he could. Still, Hutchinson could not expect Coggeshall's words to carry much influence with a body which had just stripped him of his voting rights for supporting her brother-in-law John Wheelwright.

Hutchinson's moment of truth had finally arrived on that cold November day in 1637. The deck was stacked decisively against her. Winthrop, Dudley, and the majority of the Court supported the sanctificationist ministers. The Court was determined either to "reduce" Hutchinson so that she could contribute to the good of the colony or to banish her as an incorrigible troublemaker. In this they followed a precedent established by English Protestant authorities, who often sought to reduce heretics through a combination of threats and punishments designed to turn them away from deviant opinions to Protestant orthodoxy. In Hutchinson's case this meant persuading her to renounce her allegedly "Familistical" beliefs, to admit wrongdoing in slandering the colony's ministers and godly leaders, to submit to civil authority, and to take her place as a model gentlewoman in New England society. Refusal to be reduced would mean banishment. The Court offered no middle ground.

Hutchinson brought her own agenda to the proceedings. It did not include her reduction, but a plan for defense which hinged on her contention that all she had done remained well within the legitimate boundaries of private, informal society. Her defense as it unfolded sidestepped the General Court's efforts to reduce her. Set against the backdrop of events in the late summer and fall of 1637, Hutchinson appears to have decided that her best chance for survival lay in countering that her activities lay well within the bounds of a godly gentlewoman's duties, that she only sought to pursue what Scripture commanded, and that the Court, not she, was intruding into matters of private conscience where it had no legitimate concern.

John Winthrop and the sanctificationist ministers had carefully begun to lay the groundwork for this moment the previous August, shortly after Sir Henry Vane departed the colony. Their initial targets remained the male leaders of the free grace faction who had pressed the conflict in the public arenas of church and politics. By this point they had also come to recognize Anne Hutchinson's activities within the private women's community as another important center of free grace ideas. Yet the sanctificationists could not hope to put Hutchinson herself on trial before establishing the danger of the ideas associated with her weekly meetings. They needed to persuade as many colonists as possible, Boston's teacher John Cotton included, that free grace notions posed a public danger to colonial stability.

Winthrop and Shepard joined other sanctificationist leaders in attributing much of the recent unrest to Cotton's willingness to tolerate his congregation's freewheeling theological speculation.

Yet the sanctificationist majority did not want to engage in open confrontation with a colleague who still commanded so much prestige in England and so much devotion among his own congregation in Boston. Most also genuinely respected Cotton as a man of great learning and theological insight, however inattentive he might have been to the excesses of his parishioners. Cotton's support could help the sanctificationists put a lid on the unrest in Boston while driving a wedge between him and Anne Hutchinson.

To conduct a public trial of free grace views, Winthrop persuaded the General Court to call a synod, an official gathering of all ministers and lay church officers in the colony. The ministers invited their Connecticut colleague Thomas Hooker to lend his prestige to the proceedings as a moderator of the synod along with Peter Bulkeley of Concord, Massachusetts. They invited Plymouth church leaders to participate in the synod as well. The ministers prepared carefully throughout the month of August, engaging in a series of private conferences with Cotton and Wheelwright designed to win them over to the majority. The ministers also compiled a long list of problematic beliefs suspected of emanating from Anne Hutchinson's weekly meetings. The pre-synod conferences eventually helped the ministers whittle down their differences with Cotton and Wheelwright to five key points centering on the place of faith and the witness of the Spirit in salvation and assurance. These questions they set aside for further consideration in the formal synod itself.

The trial of ideas began on August 30 as twenty-five ministers, along with elders and other elected representatives or "messengers" from the churches, gathered at the small meeting house in Newtown. The assembly of a group so admired for learning and command of the Bible attracted a large crowd of colonial observers to fill every remaining space in the building. Several of Anne Hutchinson's friends and supporters traveled from Boston, including the church's two messengers William Aspinwall and John Coggeshall.

The assembly began with an attack on free grace opinions, postponing debate with Cotton and Wheelwright. Winthrop and the sanctificationist ministers hoped to portray the ideas as unacceptably radical and unorthodox and to smoke out and isolate some of the proponents. If this succeeded, the sanctificationists' technical disputes with Cotton and Wheelwright might proceed more smoothly.

The list of reportedly dangerous ideas had grown during the pre-synod preparations to include eighty-two "erroneous opinions" and nine "unsavory speeches." All were linked by implication with the Boston church and Anne Hutchinson's weekly meetings, a number unfairly. Hutchinson herself would certainly have agreed with the first nineteen opinions listed, for example. These expressed the substance of her own passionate belief that in conversion, a believer "died to self" and became so united with Christ that her life afterward was nothing else than the direct expression of the Holy Spirit living through her—her individual personhood was wholly swallowed up in God. Hutchinson also supported opinions on the list which warned against focusing on human "gifts and graces" rather than Christ and thus becoming ensnared in a covenant of works. But she would probably have repudiated statements such as error 34, which strongly implied that a believer no longer experienced temptation or needed to pray for divine help to resist sin.

When the moderators opened the floor the following day for discussion of the "erroneous opinions," Hutchinson's allies quickly spoke up to defend many of them. Her friend John Coddington asked repeatedly whether any specific person was charged with holding one or another of the most extreme ideas. Each time, the moderators refused to name a culprit, asserting that the synod was designed to expose erroneous opinions rather than to put any person on trial. John Coggeshall and William Aspinwall joined Coddington, taking up the moderators' invitation to the audience to mount a sort of devil's advocacy of any opinions they chose.

Cotton watched the three men's performance with growing concern not only for their personal reputations but for that of the Boston church as a whole. During a break in the proceedings he pulled aside the Bostonians' two elected representatives to warn that if they really believed what they were saying, then the church in Boston would be blamed for "all these Bastardly Opinions" which other colonial churches rightly found offensive. Aspinwall and Coddington assured him that they did not necessarily accept all the disputed opinions, but they opposed a blanket condemnation of the list. They knew colonists who believed at least some of the ideas under review, and the two men did not want to bruise these "tender Consciences" by lumping a few odd but harmless ideas together with serious doctrinal errors.

Aspinwall's and Coddington's reply forced Cotton to realize for the first time that some of the "tender Consciences" in his congregation, including Anne Hutchinson herself, might genuinely cherish "these Bastardly Opinions." The lively and sometimes heated theological debates which occupied his congregation had signaled, not just a taste for speculation, but a "real and broad difference" between the ideas of those who favored "Mistris *Hutchinson*" and those of Cotton himself.

Cotton's sudden recognition of the gulf between his views and Hutchinson's prompted him to take a public stand against the whole list of opinions, much to the dismay of those in Hutchinson's circle. "Some of the Opinions," he told the synod, were blasphemous, some heretical, many erroneous, and almost all "incommodiously expressed." In the wake of Cotton's declaration, Aspinwall and Coddington withdrew from the synod and went home along with several other Bostonians.

With Hutchinson's supporters gone, the synod worked quickly down the list, condemning all errors and authorizing a written refutation of each. The sanctificationist Thomas Weld later compared the result to a litter of ninety-one "brats hung up against the sun." Just as authorities of the time tied petty criminals to a pillory in the center of town to suffer the community's stares and jeers, so the errors of Anne Hutchinson's circle were aired in shameful public display.

Having branded as false doctrine the views attributed to the free grace faction, the synod turned to the task of reconciling Cotton's and Wheelwright's views with those of the sanctificationists. The previous week's debate had persuaded Cotton that a real problem existed, and he was ready to deal. One by one, Cotton forged a compromise on the disputed points which remained from the pre-synod debates among the ministers, and each concession drove a deeper doctrinal wedge between himself and Anne Hutchinson. Wheelwright, on the other hand, remained convinced that the greater danger to gospel truth remained with the sanctificationists rather than himself and the partisans of free grace. He remained adamant in his own views, refusing to make concessions as Cotton had done. In so doing he sealed his isolation from Cotton and the rest of the colonial ministerial community.

The public trial of ideas had achieved Governor Winthrop's aims. The synod had pilloried a long list of beliefs suspected of spreading from Anne Hutchinson's weekly meetings. It had patched together a fragile accommodation between Cotton and the sanctificationist majority. On its final day, the synod capped off its work by passing a set of resolutions aimed directly at Hutchinson and her followers. The assembly condemned the free grace faction's disruptive habits of hostile questioning during sermons and leaving their home congregations over minor differences in doctrine. They resolved that the civil officers possessed the rightful authority to suppress such disorders. They condemned Hutchinson's bi-weekly meetings. Small groups of women might profitably meet for "prayer and edification," synod members acknowledged. Yet Hutchinson's meetings were disorderly and transgressed what the Bible allowed. They were too big and too regular—attracting sixty or more every week—and were led by a lone woman who posed as a prophet by "resolving questions of doctrine, and expounding scripture."

The synod's concluding resolutions paved the way for Winthrop to prosecute his final campaign against Anne Hutchinson and the party of free grace. On September 26, four days after the synod adjourned, the General Court also adjourned and its members went home. During the next few weeks, several of the towns chose new deputies to represent them at the court's upcoming autumn meeting. The Court which met at the beginning of November included fifteen deputies who had not sat in the August session—nearly half the total thirty-two. The overall majority was even more hostile than the last toward "those who leaned to Mistris Hutchinson."

Hutchinson's actions in late September and October indicate that she rejected the synod's actions and remained determined to advance her views through all means available to a puritan woman of Boston. She continued to pack sixty visitors into her house at her weekly meetings. When Winthrop criticized Cotton for winking at this evident defiance of the synod, the minister simply replied that Boston's elders had received no credible report of heresy or disorder in her meetings. This suggests that Hutchinson had toned things down somewhat. Even so, inexplicable female disorders also continued to strike Hutchinson and several women friends whenever John Wilson entered the pulpit, prompting them to stand and walk out of the meetinghouse.

If Cotton remained willing to tolerate Hutchinson's conduct, Winthrop's patience had reached its end. The governor determined to follow his Connecticut friend Thomas Hooker's advice to strike the free grace faction so suddenly and decisively that its members would despair of preventing or resisting the move.

Cotton must have wondered whether God had beaten Winthrop to the punch when a distressed Anne Hutchinson knocked on her teacher's door late on the night of October 17. Her story tumbled out as Cotton led her inside. She had come from the bedside of her friend Mary Dyer, who had just delivered a still-born "monster," an infant with multiple birth defects which probably included anacephaly (lack of a cerebrum) and spina bifida (an incompletely formed spinal cord). As John Winthrop later described it, Dyer's "woman child" possessed a face "but no head," with ears "upon the shoulders" and shaped "like an ape's." It had no forehead, "but over the eyes four horns, hard and sharp." Its eyes popped out, "and the mouth also; the nose hooked upward." Its body was covered with "sharp pricks and scales," reminiscent of the rays sometimes caught in fishermen's nets. Its navel, belly, and genitals seemed to be on the wrong side and "the back and hips . . . where the belly should have been." Between its shoulders two "mouths" appeared with a "piece of red flesh" protruding from each. It had normal arms and legs, but "instead of toes, it had on each foot three claws, like a young fowl, with sharp talons."

Cotton listened to Hutchinson's story with mingled sympathy and alarm. He clearly recognized the voice of God in this portent, but what did the message mean? Cotton knew as well as Hutchinson that in the context of the recent synod's actions, the sanctificationist majority would interpret this "monstrous birth" as a sign of God's wrath upon the entire Hutchinson circle. Indeed, Governor John Winthrop concluded exactly that when he got wind of the event several months later. Both knew that news of the birth would turn the entire colony even more firmly against the free grace faction in Boston.

The two rehearsed the evening's events in an effort to discern God's will. To them, the circumstances of the birth suggested that God had sent a private message to the Dyers, not a proclamation to the entire colony. After all, no one had been in the room at the moment of birth except Hutchinson, the midwife Jane Hawkins, and one other woman who had pledged silence. Hutchinson had not yet even told Mary, who had passed out from pain, grief, and exhaustion as soon as her labor ceased. William Dyer still remained in the dark as well. Perhaps no one but the parents needed to know. That is certainly what Cotton would have preferred, he told Hutchinson, if his own wife had been in Mary Dyer's place. Better simply to report the baby stillborn and remain silent about the details, musing privately on the lessons God might intend for the parents and the witnesses. Hutchinson eventually departed, comforted by her teacher's words and the regard they conveyed for her and her circle of friends.

If God's purposes in Mary Dyer's "monstrous birth" proved mystifying to those who kept her secret, John Winthrop's actions three weeks later were unambiguous. He and other leading magistrates had decided that the Hutchinson circle's defiance of the synod had made the colony's situation "desperate." Colonial officials must act without further delay to suppress the "troublers of our peace." As soon as the newly elected General Court convened in Newtown on November 2, it began issuing summons to several "erroneous and seditious persons for their disturbance of the publick peace."

The Court's unfinished business with Hutchinson's brother-in-law John Wheelwright provided Winthrop the pretext he needed to act against her circle. The General Court had long ago convicted Wheelwright of sedition but not yet sentenced him. Neither had it yet responded definitively to the petition on Wheelwright's behalf which had been signed by scores of supporters from Boston. Hutchinson's name was not among the signatures since women did not sign petitions, but that did not matter to Winthrop. The hospitality she extended to the male signatories and their families would provide sufficient pretext for the governor to summon her too.

When Wheelwright appeared before the General Court, Winthrop cut straight to the chase. Was the fiery minister prepared to acknowledge his offense or did he prefer to let the Court pass its long-deferred sentence? Wheelwright retorted that he had committed "no sedition or contempt." He had spoken nothing but the "truth of Christ." Winthrop reminded him that his Fast Day Sermon had clearly implied that most of the colony's ministers were "enemies to Christ, and Antichrists." Moreover, the results of the sermon had been to divide the colony into factions, turning everything "upside down among us." Wheelwright remained defiant, declaring that with God's help, he would prove by Scripture the things he had taught.

Wheelwright had made his choice: he would let the Court pass its sentence. Even so, the Court spent a second day and part of a third wrangling with the minister over whether he would leave voluntarily and whether he might appeal his sentence to the King. Finally, on the morning of the third day, Wheelwright bowed to the Court's judgment. He could no longer remain in the colony without destroying it. He was therefore disfranchised—stripped of his right to vote and hold office in the colony—and commanded to leave Massachusetts Bay by the end of the following March. They also commanded him not to preach. When Wheelwright refused, they ordered him out in two weeks. His wife and family spent the winter at Mount Wollaston, where they prepared to join him in New Hampshire the following spring.

In sentencing Wheelwright, the General Court threw down the gauntlet to the free grace faction: submit or accept the consequences. The magistrates reinforced that message by convicting and sentencing two of Hutchinson's closest associates, John Coggeshall and William Aspinwall, whom the Court charged as ringleaders of the dissention which had threatened the public peace. They were tried for signing the *Remonstrance or Petition* the previous March which protested Wheelwright's earlier conviction. Cogshall was disfranchised, but saved himself from banishment by moderating his speech and behavior to a much more respectful level before the Court's authority. The Court disfranchised Aspinwall, an affront which the fiery drafter of the

March petition did not take lying down. His boisterous response aggravated the Court so greatly that it banished him from the colony as well.

By the time Anne Hutchinson stepped into the Newtown meeting house on November 7, the campaign against the free grace faction had developed significant momentum. Hutchinson probably had to face the Court alone. Neither her husband William nor any of her sons appear in the records of her trial before the General Court, though they may have stood as silent observers of the proceedings. Winthrop may have calculated that after four days of successful convictions, this Court composed of the colony's leading men would sweep away a lone woman with little resistance. He did not reckon sufficiently with Hutchinson's eloquence and resourcefulness.

Winthrop opened the trial with a summary of charges against Hutchinson. Despite the governor's prejudice, he recognized that members of the General Court—as well as the populace of Massachusetts Bay—would recognize the legitimacy of any censure only if Hutchinson was duly convicted of a legal offense. This required him to cast her actions as public, political affronts to the court's authority rather than the private, informal functions of a gentlewoman. He therefore recited three primary accusations. Hutchinson was "joined in affinity and affection" with those already convicted. She had "spoken diverse things . . . very prejudicial to the honour of the churches and ministers thereof." She had "maintained a meeting and an assembly" in her house which had been condemned by the General Court. Now he wanted to know whether Hutchinson supported John Wheelwright's Fast Day Sermon and the petition submitted in Wheelwright's defense. These offenses had already gotten John Coggeshall disfranchised and William Aspinwall banished.

Hutchinson knew better than to take this bait. She countered that she had heard "no things laid to my charge," essentially denying that any of Winthrop's three main accusations constituted actual violations of the law. In effect, she was claiming that all three remained well within the private arena of a gentlewoman's legitimate duties. Hutchinson had said or done nothing worthy of public censure. Winthrop retorted that Hutchinson had indeed committed chargeable offenses, the first of which involved her choice to continue associating with and offering hospitality to the leaders of the campaign to petition on Wheelwright's behalf. Her association with these lawbreakers made her an accessory to their crimes.

Hutchinson's response unfolded in a string of verbal thrusts and parries with the governor in which she performed brilliantly. As her defense unfolded, a counter-narrative to Winthrop's began to emerge. While her own actions remained legitimately confined to the spheres of informal colonial society, Winthrop's arbitrary public measures had wrongly intruded into the private arena. Hutchinson countered that her extension of hospitality to the petitioners had been a "matter of conscience," that is, private and non-political. She had not entertained them as lawbreakers but as "saints"—fellow Christians who had experienced conversion and were members in the same church as she. Winthrop retorted that since the petitioners had broken the law, anyone who entertained them for conscience sake was also guilty as an accessory to their crimes. Hutchinson denied that she had made any possible lawbreaking a matter of conscience. She had not signed the petition protesting Wheelwright's conviction, nor had she welcomed her brother-in-law and others such as Coggeshall and Aspinwall as members of any faction. She had entertained them only as fellow Christians, something any other good Christian was bound by conscience to do.

With this assertion, Hutchinson backed Winthrop into a corner. He and many others sitting with him in the General Court had followed the same distinction as she. They, too, had continued to associate with members of the petition signers as "them that fear the Lord"—as much a matter of conscience for them as for Hutchinson. They had served together in church assemblies, dined together in each others' homes, ministered to each other during illness or childbirth, or harvested crops shoulder to shoulder. To convict Hutchinson of a practice so many of the General Court had followed would amount to rank hypocrisy. Frustrated, the governor lashed out that he did "not mean to discourse with those of your sex" except to insist that by associating with the petition signers "you do dishonor" the Massachusetts Bay authorities. Winthrop's outburst certainly carried the implication that Hutchinson was transgressing a gender boundary by engaging in public debate with him over the legal implications of her actions. Hutchinson neatly parried the implication, however, refusing to acknowledge that she "ever put any dishonour upon you."

Hutchinson's response brought to a close the first charge of "harbouring and countenancing" the petitioners. Winthrop tacitly conceded defeat by shifting to a new charge, the legality of her weekly meetings. Why, he asked, did Hutchinson hold "such a meeting at your house as you do every week upon a set day?"

To Anne Hutchinson, the answer seemed obvious: it was as legal for her to hold her meetings as it was for Winthrop and everyone else in the room who held such meetings in their own homes. Indeed, she had only begun her meetings after other colonial women had chided her for pride and neglect of this useful method of spiritual observance. Other colonists had persuaded her that such gatherings were "lawful," or permitted by the Bible, leading her to wonder whether Winthrop could find scriptural justification "for yourself and condemn me for the same thing?"

Hutchinson's reply set off an exchange with the governor which revealed a surprising degree of common ground between their views on the Bible's teaching about women's religious roles. They diverged, however, on the question of how biblical teaching applied to the public/private distinctions within seventeenth century practice. Winthrop first argued that Hutchinson had violated biblical gender norms by welcoming men to her meetings. Hutchinson did not disagree that to do so would "cross a rule" of Scripture. She denied, however, that men ever attended the meetings where she actually taught. She later explained that her family sometimes hosted mixed meetings taught only by men. She also admitted discussing theological matters with men, but only in response to private inquiry between brother and sister in the Lord, never as teacher—a distinction Winthrop grudgingly accepted. She drew scriptural justification for her teaching of women from the command of Titus 2:3–5 that "the elder women should instruct the younger."

Hutchinson's invocation of this passage undercut Winthrop's argument, for he shared her belief that Titus 2 commanded women to meet for such purposes. Even so, he pressed on to challenge the *manner* of her meetings. Their timing and format had the disorderly effect of drawing "a company together from their callings to be taught" by Hutchinson. The historian Mary Beth Norton has argued that Winthrop drew a distinction between private, occasional meetings which Titus 2:3–5 might permit a woman to lead and public meetings which he defined as such by their size and regularity. In this view, Hutchinson's meetings fell in the latter category and made her leadership illegitimate in spite of what the passage in question might say. In addition, Winthrop believed that any meeting, public or private, should promote communal harmony rather than the disorder he detected in any practice which distracted people from their callings.

Winthrop had chosen a slippery course and lost his footing quickly. Hutchinson rejected his view that her meetings were public, as did other influential members of the General Court. Where in the Bible, she wanted to know, could Winthrop find a principle of conduct which permitted her to turn away those who came to her for instruction? She had already shown him very clear justification for receiving such inquirers. Once again, the governor found himself on the defensive and losing more ground with every statement. Hutchinson's course was "prejudicial to the state," he declared. Her meetings turned people against "magistrates and ministers." They seduced mothers into neglecting their families. They wasted precious time. "We see not," he fumed, "that any should have authority to set up any other exercises besides what authority hath already set up."

Hutchinson had teased from Winthrop a very unpuritan invocation of naked magisterial power against a Christian practice clearly commanded in the Bible. Many sitting in the Newtown meeting house that day had left homes and families in England precisely because the authorities had banned conventicles such as Hutchinson's. They would not follow Winthrop onto this dangerous ground.

Hutchinson pressed her advantage with a display of womanly meekness which contrasted sharply with Winthrop's authoritarianism. She volunteered to suspend her meetings as "a free will offering" in token of her submission. Deputy Simon Bradstreet quickly objected. Hutchinson ought not do a thing so offensive to the puritan community. To disband her gatherings—even voluntarily—would set an alarming precedent, making all such meetings in the colony illegal in principle and rendering guilty all women who continued to meet in private homes for Bible study and prayer. "I am not against all women's meetings," Bradstreet concluded, perhaps with a meaningful glance toward Winthrop, "but consider them lawful."

As deputy governor Thomas Dudley watched Hutchinson deal Winthrop this second defeat, his patience snapped. Perhaps to rescue the case from the governor's fumbling, Dudley interjected with the Court's most damning indictment: Hutchinson had disparaged nearly every minister in the colony by claiming that they "preached a covenant of works, and only Mr. Cotton a covenant of grace." Here, stated in the starkest terms, was the issue which had riven the colony for the past two years.

Dudley's accusation had shifted Hutchinson to very treacherous ground, and the General Court held her there from this point forward. Hutchinson had indeed drawn an unfavorable distinction between the other Bay Colony ministers and Cotton, a point she never denied. Indeed, she declared to Dudley that if she had ever characterized other ministers as less able than Cotton, she "proved it by God's word." Her hope of refuting this accusation seemed especially slim as six of those disparaged ministers prepared to recite what they remembered of their conference with her about this matter more than a year before. Hutchinson's main line of defense continued to hew to the public/private distinction. She insisted that since she had spoken privately to the ministers in that meeting, it had not been in any sense official or public, and they had no business repeating the conversation. Their testimony was inadmissible. By pouring all her wit and eloquence into this line of defense, she kept her case alive for the remainder of the first day's examination and well into the second.

To be sure, the rest of the first day's examination did not go especially well for Hutchinson. Beginning with Salem's pastor Hugh Peter, the ministers testified in turn that she had asserted that a "wide and a broad difference" stood between Cotton and the rest of the colony's ministers. Peter acknowledged that their conference with Hutchinson had been conducted in private among friends rather than as a public judicial matter. For this reason, the ministers were reluctant to answer except that the

Court now commanded them to speak. Even so, Peter recalled that when pressed to "clear herself and deal plainly," Hutchinson did not ask them to hold her statements in confidence or to shield her from their consequences. He accordingly asserted that she had said that Cotton preached "a covenant of grace and you a covenant of works." They were "not able ministers of the new testament." They knew "no more than the apostles did before the resurrection of Christ" because they had not received "the seal of the spirit," the inner witness which provided true assurance of conversion.

The combined testimony of six ministers confronted Hutchinson with a formidable challenge, but Deputy Governor Dudley's penchant for overstatement gave her the toehold she needed to keep her defense alive. In addition to questioning the ministers' fitness for office, Dudley charged, she held questionable views about the Bible itself. He tried to put a Familistical spin on her ideas asserting that she claimed the scriptures "in the letter of them held nothing but a covenant of works" and that those "under a covenant of works" could not be saved. Dudley was essentially claiming that Hutchinson secretly rejected the authority of the written Bible and took spiritual guidance from inward revelations alone. He also argued that Hutchinson had forfeited her right to insist on the privacy of her conference with the ministers because she had not spoken as a friend in confidence. Instead, she had invoked her conscience as the reason for her statement about the ministers. She had prefaced her remarks by declaring "the fear of man is a snare wherefore should I be afraid, I will speak plainly and freely." In Dudley's view, this declaration gave her subsequent observations the force of a formal challenge to the ministers' authority as guardians of truth and reliable spiritual guides. Such a challenge called into question the spiritual well-being of every church and every person in the colony who sat under these ministers. She must either vindicate it or recant in public.

Hutchinson denied two of Dudley's assertions. She retorted that the deputy governor had put words in her mouth about the Bible which she did not actually hold. She denied believing that the gospel "in letter and words" taught only a covenant of works. Hutchinson revered and sought to live by the written

Word of God. She also denied that she had drawn her distinctions between Cotton and other ministers as a point of conscience rather than in friendship. She had made her declaration about the "fear of man" very late in the conference. She expanded upon these two denials until the end of the first day's trial, challenging details of the ministers' statements with her own alternative account of the order in which the conference had proceeded.

As dusk began to gather outside the Newtown meeting house, Winthrop intervened to call a recess. Although Hutchinson had embarrassed him in the first two exchanges of the day, the testimony of the six ministers seemed to restore his confidence in the way the examination was proceeding. The governor closed by observing how the court had labored to persuade Hutchinson "to acknowledge the error of your way so that you might be reduced." She should take a little more time to think about it that evening before returning to court the next day.

Hutchinson did think about the day's exchange after returning home to Boston that evening, but not as Winthrop intended. Instead, she reviewed Pastor John Wilson's own notes of her conference with the ministers (these notes have since been lost) and found that the interview had not transpired exactly as the six pastors had described it. The next morning she opened her defense with a legal maneuver, throwing the court into confusion which occupied much of the day. She charged the ministers with testifying the previous day "in their own cause," an accusation of prejudice. For her, the issue remained the timing of her declaration that she would disregard "the fear of man" to speak "plainly and freely." The ministers had invoked that statement to justify breaking confidence to testify against her the previous day. She hoped to prove that these were not her first words, and that this would make the ministers' testimony inadmissible in Court. In light of their prejudice and the discrepancies she had found between their testimony and Wilson's record, the Court should require them to testify upon oath.

Hutchinson's accusers continued to regard the order of her statements as merely incidental. Yet if the Court required them to swear an oath to their memory of such trivial details, their imperfect recall might result in an inadvertent misstatement of fact and so cause them to commit perjury, a very serious sin before God as well as a very serious crime. Winthrop extended them a lifeline by pointing out that as a high court, the General Court did not try by jury, so oaths were not required. Straight testimony would suffice unless some members of the Court or the colony refused to accept it otherwise. Several members replied that only an oath would satisfy them. The fiercely independent Israel Stoughton of Dorchester declared he would abstain from any vote to censure Hutchinson if the ministers refused.

Deputy Governor Dudley finally broke the impasse by calling forward three witnesses who had also been at the meeting and could testify in Hutchinson's defense. Her friend John Coggeshall testified that Hutchinson did not say everything the ministers had alleged. Boston elder Thomas Leverett recalled her saying only that "they did not preach a covenant of grace so clearly as Mr. Cotton did." John Cotton concluded his own lengthy testimony by observing that at the time, her accusers had not taken Hutchinson's distinction between himself and them so ill as they were now taking it. He recalled that they had indeed promised to "they would speak no more of it." This supported Hutchinson's contention that they had breached confidence by testifying publicly. Cotton added that he "did not find her saying they were under a covenant of works, nor that she said they did preach a covenant of works."

In the end, however, the testimony of the three defense witnesses was not enough to exonerate Hutchinson. None of the three had refuted the claim that Hutchinson had questioned the ministers' ability to preach the Gospel, the main substance of Deputy Governor Dudley's charge. The other matters were incidental. "Mr. Cotton hath expressed what he remembered and what took an impression upon him," Winthrop observed, "and so I think the other elders also did remember that which took an impression upon them." Seventeenth-century courts of justice encountered this sort of mildly conflicting testimony all the time, but enough had been said to demonstrate that Hutchinson had indeed made unflattering statements about the ministers. Hutchinson's privacy defense had collapsed. It was a serious offense in the seventeenth century to "traduce" a public person. It not only violated standards of conduct but was seen to undercut that person's authority and in this case had caused months of public disorder. In England an offender could be fined, jailed, or maimed. Here in Massachusetts, Hutchinson faced banishment for her crime.

At this point, Hutchinson jolted the Court by offering to explain exactly why she knew her assertions about the sanctificationist ministers were true. She recalled that, while still living in England, she had set aside a "day of solemn humiliation" to consider whether to escape the unbiblical ceremonies and government of the English Church by "turning separatist"—leaving the Church of England, as the Pilgrims in Plymouth had done. As she pondered, the words of I John 2:18 came to mind, "He that denies Jesus Christ to be come in the flesh is antichrist." But how could this verse help her? Neither the Church of England priests nor the very Pope in Rome denied this. She asked God to intervene with supernatural guidance and remove her confusion with further Scriptural insight. This the Lord did by reminding her of Hebrews 9:16, "He that denies the testament denies the testator."

Hutchinson explained that this passage helped her to see that those who did not teach the new testament—which she understood as the free grace views she had learned from Wheelwright and Cotton—"had the spirit of antichrist." Ever since that day, she had been able to detect which minister was right and which was wrong. She could distinguish between the "voice of my beloved"—Jesus himself—and the voice of Moses—the Covenant of Works as expressed in the Ten Commandments. She could also identify the "voice of John Baptist"—the imperfect preaching of the Covenant of Grace by those not yet sealed by the Spirit—and the "spirit of antichrist"—papists, Church of England priests, perhaps even some sanctificationist ministers. This was how Hutchinson knew that none of the Bay Colony ministers preached the Covenant of Grace as clearly as did John Cotton. If the Court was going to condemn her for speaking "what in my conscience I know to be truth, I must commit myself unto the Lord."

Here at last, spoken plainly in open court, was Hutchinson's direct declaration of unfavorable distinctions among various ministers—along with a hint of an idea much more disturbing. Increase Nowell probed deeper: "How do you know that that was the spirit," he asked, who had led Hutchinson to this conclusion?

In answer to Nowell's query, Hutchinson drew on the well-known biblical account in which God told Abraham to sacrifice his son Isaac as a burnt offering. "How did Abraham know that it was God that bid him offer his son," she retorted, especially when the request entailed a violation of the command not to commit murder? "By an immediate voice," Deputy Governor Dudley replied, an answer that every child knew. "So to me by an immediate revelation," Hutchinson declared.

"How! An immediate revelation?" Dudley's astonished outburst gave voice to the consternation that swept across the meeting house. Did Anne Hutchinson really believe that God spoke directly to her just as he had spoken to Abraham and other Old Testament prophets? Her claim seemed to mark a radical break from standard puritan observance. She was comparing her spiritual experience to that of the Bible's male prophets and heroes of the faith. Few puritans would have dared to draw such a parallel. Even leading men such as John Winthrop wrote of their spiritual journeys in feminine terms, drawing examples from biblical women whose stories of faith stressed uncertainty, weakness, and utter dependence on the Lord.

Hutchinson's next retort poured fuel on the fire: the Lord had spoken "by the voice of his own spirit to my soul." This seemed to dispense with the Bible as the rule of faith, even though she went on to explain how the Lord spoke by bringing scriptures to her mind. He had comforted her thus after Cotton and Wheelwright had been forced from Lincolnshire. Similarly, when Hutchinson resolved to come to New England, a passage from the prophet Isaiah kept returning to her mind to suggest that she would find affliction in her new home. Yet another recurrent passage from Daniel balanced the first. There the Lord assured her that if affliction came, he was the same God who delivered Daniel from "the lion's den, I will also deliver thee."

Hutchinson paused and drew herself up to pronounce a dire warning. The prophecy of affliction she had received through the verse in Isaiah was now coming to pass, and the General Court was its instrument. The Court may hold "power over my body," she cautioned, "but the Lord Jesus hath power over my body and soul." Hutchinson expected God's protection to bring her safely through her affliction, but she did not think the members of the Court would fare so well if they voted to convict her. Indeed, such an action would place them on the wrong side of the spiritual battle over the colony and to "put the Lord Jesus Christ from you." It would "bring a curse upon you and your posterity, and the mouth of the Lord hath spoken it."

With this pronouncement, Hutchinson handed the shocked members of the General Court all the evidence they needed to pronounce their harshest censure upon her. Why she did so has puzzled historians, who have alternately attributed her outburst to nervous exhaustion, illness, or prophetic ecstasy. The historian Mary Beth Norton has rejected these explanations to argue that Hutchinson made a conscious decision at the end of her defense to cross the line and make a public attempt to persuade the Court of the truth of her views. The historian Michael Winship adds that in doing so, she fulfilled a promise she had made earlier in the day to "explain why she knew the elders of the Bay were not able ministers of the New Testament." Or perhaps, once her defense collapsed, Hutchinson simply concluded that she had nothing more to lose and fell back on the only remaining argument she could think of. Perhaps she thought there was an outside chance of intimidating the Court with threats of divine judgment. If not, she would go down fighting for her convictions.

Hutchinson's claim of direct revelation apparently blind-sided her teacher John Cotton, yet he intervened in a last-ditch effort to rescue her from censure. He tried to distinguish between two "sorts of revelations." The sort which came without reference to the Bible and sometimes contradicted it was a figment of the imagination and dangerous "in more ways than one." A second sort, however, was "breathed by the spirit of God." It never came except in a passage of Scripture, and it always agreed with Scripture. If Cotton understood Hutchinson correctly, she was claiming the second, not the first. The historian Michael Dittmore has argued that Cotton did correctly understand her. She detected God's voice in scripture by the method her teacher summarized in her defense, one which he himself had taught.

John Winthrop had no patience for Cotton's efforts to rescue Hutchinson. Her claim to revelation had transformed her case. It would "not stand with us now," the governor declared. A "marvelous providence of God" had prompted her to reveal clearly what some members had suspected all along: spurious ideas of divine revelation lay behind "all these disturbances." Deputy Governor Dudley recalled that just such ideas had prompted the Germans in Muenster to "take up arms against their prince and to cut the throats one of another." Winthrop swept aside Cotton's defense of Hutchinson to proclaim that her revelations were the first kind—the dangerous, classical Familist sort which came through "the immediate revelation of the spirit and not by the ministry of the word." Hutchinson's revelations had formed the root "of all these tumults and troubles," Winthrop concluded, and he closed with the wish that everyone who had troubled the colony were "cut off from us." As the governor fell silent, the Court replied in chorus "we all consent with you."

The Court's expression of consent marked the effective end of the trial. A few deputies continued to insist on hearing sworn testimony from at least two of Hutchinson's ministerial accusers before they would vote to censure her, so John Eliot and Hugh Peter did so. This formality accomplished, Winthrop called for a vote of censure. If the members agreed that Mrs. Hutchinson was "unfit for our society" and should be "banished out of our liberties and imprisoned until she be sent away," the governor said, "let them hold up their hands." William Jennison of Watertown abstained. All others except the Boston representatives voted in favor.

Winthrop turned to Hutchinson and pronounced the sentence: "You are banished from out of our jurisdiction as being a woman not fit for our society, and are to be imprisoned until the court shall send you away."

"I desire to know wherefore I am banished?" Hutchinson replied.

"Say no more," Winthrop ordered. "The court knows and is satisfied."

"A Dayngerus Instrument of the Divell"

In early March 1640, three visitors from Boston tramped through the snow to the door of Anne and William Hutchinson's newly constructed house in the fledgling town of Portsmouth on Aquidneck, soon to be renamed Rhode Island. After William had admitted them, the three explained that they had come from the church in Boston to check on the spiritual state of the church's "wandering sheep" who had departed following the examinations and censures two years before. William replied that he considered himself "more nearly tied to his wife than to the church" in Boston. He continued to regard her a "dear saint and servant of god."

The three then asked to speak with "mrs Hutchison." When she entered, they told her they had a message for her "from the Lord and from our church." She responded warily that there were many lords and many gods, but "I acknowledge but one Lord. Which Lord doe you mean?" The three replied that they "came in the Name but of one Lord and that is god." Here at least was a small point of agreement, Hutchinson observed, "and where we do agree, Let it be set downe."

Neither Hutchinson's enigmatic response nor the "disdaine in her countenance" offered the messengers much encouragement. Even so, they pressed on to declare that they had a message to her "from the church of christ in Boston."

"What, from the *Church* at *Boston*?" she exclaimed. "I know no such *Church*, neither will I owne it. Call it the *Whore and Strumpet* of *Boston*, no Church of Christ."

Hutchinson's fierce reply exuded a bitterness unabated from her humiliating banishment from Boston in the winter of 1637–1638. She had poured more than three years of her life into helping to build a church and society where her family and neighbors could live under the pure ministry of Godly pastors and teachers. Now she and her family found themselves in exile on the wild shore of Aquidneck Island, trying to scrape together the remnants of their hopes and dreams along with a few others who no longer found a welcome in Massachusetts Bay.

Hutchinson's bitter ordeal in Boston left her with wounds that probably never healed. Her pursuit of godliness after her exile took her into regions of belief and practice where even many of her closest friends and supporters from Boston were unwilling to follow, leading her to increasing isolation and eventual death on frontiers of neighboring Dutch New Netherlands. A watchful John Winthrop kept tabs on Hutchinson's movements during the next five years, noting in his diary whenever news filtered back to Boston concerning her activities and influence. For him, as for many others, her life in the years after her exile from Boston vindicated the judgment of the General Court and the Church of Boston that she had been a *"dayngerus Instrument of the Divell* raysed up by Sathan amongst us to rayse up Divissions and Contentions"* and to alienate the colonists from one from another.

To be sure, it took the majority in Boston several months to unite around that conclusion. Anne Hutchinson's sentence of banishment initially sparked an outcry among the members of the Boston church, many of whom were "highly offended" with Winthrop for the leading role he had played in her examination before the General Court. Although Winthrop delivered a public defense of his conduct before the congregation, the discontent persisted throughout the winter months. Indeed, the resentment that seethed among members of Hutchinson's circle made the members of the General Court fear that Dudley's observation at her trial might come true: a New England John of Leyden might arise with a claim of divine revelation to lead an armed uprising and kill all the magistrates. The Court acted swiftly to head off such a possibility by ordering that anyone who had signed the *Remonstrance or Petition* be disarmed.

The Court sent the constables a list of seventy-five petition signers with an order that each should surrender all "guns, pistols, swords, powder, shot, & match" within ten days or face a stiff ten-pound fine. Each defendant could avoid the order, however, by humbly appearing before the General Court to "acknowledge his sinn in subscribing to the seditious libel." Within a few days, thirty men appeared, hats in hand, to submit and request their names be stricken from the petition. Another five protested that their names had been added without their consent. The rest reluctantly handed in their weapons.

As the grumbling over these actions continued through the winter months, members of Hutchinson's extended family often trekked across the snow from Boston to the town of Roxbury, where she was under house arrest until her March departure. They returned to Boston with reports that she was advocating disturbing new religious ideas which were infecting other colonists. The reports prompted John Cotton to spend the next several months ferreting out such beliefs among members of his congregation and urging proponents to renounce them.

While Cotton busied himself tracking down unorthodox ideas among his Boston congregation, other colonial ministers braved the deep winter snows to confer with Anne Hutchinson at Roxbury. During their visits they learned that she persisted in the "gross errors" which had been coming to light in Boston. Thomas Shepard spearheaded a request to the Boston church to expose her deviant views in a public examination before the entire congregation. The church complied, and Hutchinson was given a license to appear before the congregation on March 15, 1638.

While Hutchinson's civil examination had aimed at reducing her to become a profitable member of colonial society, her church trial focused on reducing her from theological error to orthodoxy. Churches in colonial Massachusetts exercised discipline to restore wayward members to common standards of religious belief and moral practice and to promote harmony within the congregation. In this sense, reduction functioned as sort of doctrinal and moral rehabilitation which depended on the "humiliation" of the transgressor—that is, her voluntary, humble repentance from the specified fault and her meek submission to the church leadership's loving correction. In Hutchinson's case, reduction through her church trial would not lift her banishment any more than a murderer's reduction would allow him to escape the gallows. It would, however, restore her to fellowship, permitting the Boston church to send her away with its blessing and to offer her family spiritual support as they sought to establish a church in their new home.

If efforts to reduce Hutchinson failed, however, she would be excommunicated—cut off "as a Hethen and a Publican" from participation in the sacrament of the Lord's Supper and from the communal life and support of her fellow Christians in Boston. Yet even this drastic action was intended to drive the subject to repentance and restoration, and it frequently succeeded. The case of Anne Hett was one such success story. She was excommunicated from the Boston church in 1642 after attempting to kill her child in a fit of despair over her own salvation. According to John Winthrop, the experience penetrated her depression after all other methods had failed. Before long, her sincere expression of repentance and return to emotional stability prompted the church to restore her to full membership.

The church trial began on Thursday, March 15, the Boston church's weekly lecture day. After the conclusion of the customary sermon, a weary Anne Hutchinson, weakened from more than three months' confinement, was led to a seat at the front of the assembly. Her husband William had already left Massachusetts Bay to scout a new home site for his soon-to-be-exiled family. Her grown son Edward and her son-in-law Thomas Savage, however, both remained members of the Boston church and sat in the congregation as participants in the trial.

Boston elder Thomas Leverett opened the proceedings by reading her a list of sixteen deviant opinions compiled by Thomas Shepard and an elder in Shepard's church. Some were well known from her earlier trial, but the list also included a new set of opinions challenging a central tenet of traditional Christian orthodoxy: the final resurrection of the body.

This charged raised great concern among colonial leaders. Reverend Zechariah Symmes observed that if news got back to England that people were raising questions about such a core belief, it would be one of the "greatest Dishonours to Jesus Christ and of Reproch to thease Churches." The news might invite vigorous intervention from ecclesiastical authorities in England. If this were not enough, a Familist version of this belief reputedly taught that a spiritual resurrection actually occurred at conversion. This supposedly restored the convert to innocence and liberated him or her from any fleshly moral constraints, including marriage. The idea was thought to form the basis of "the community of women," a seventeenth-century form of free love.

The views Shepard charged against Hutchinson did not exactly match the Familist model, although they clearly deviated from traditional orthodoxy. Hutchinson had privately told Shepard that she believed human souls to be mortal and subject to simple annihilation—passing out of existence—at death unless a person became "united with Christ" through personal faith. She also questioned whether biblical passages concerning the resurrection of believers referred simply to "Union with Christ Jesus," and not physical resurrection of the dead believers' remains.

Hutchinson shook off her weariness to meet these charges with the same canny eloquence she had displayed in her civil examination. Indeed, she opened her defense with the very same accusation against Shepard which had nearly confounded the prosecution at the earlier trial: Shepard, like her previous ministerial accusers, had violated a sort of minister-client privilege by making her statements public before he had "privately delt with me." Shepard and the Boston church, however, must have anticipated this line of attack and quickly put it to rest by explaining that the minister had in fact borne ample private "witness against" her opinions before calling her before the church. Hutchinson then fell back on a second line of defense, declaring that *she* had not actually committed herself to many of these beliefs; she was only raising questions. This opened a lengthy debate which occupied the remainder of her first day's trial.

Hutchinson's defense is very interesting for the light it sheds on how this gifted, literate lay woman approached her reading of the Bible and attempted to make sense of its often enigmatic statements. The transcript of her debate with the ministers reveals a woman very much at home with the text of her scriptures and very much in her element as a debater of their meaning.

Hutchinson's questions about the mortality of the soul arose from her reading of two specific passages, Ecclesiastes 3:18–21 and Hebrews 4:12. A straightforward reading of the first suggested the idea to Hutchinson with its striking parallel description of the death of humans and beasts: "as one dies, so dies the other, for they have all one breath, and there is no excellence of man above the beast. . . . who knows whether the spirit of man ascends upward, and the spirit of the beast descend downward to the earth?" Hutchinson knew from listening to many puritan sermons and lectures that "breath" was the root meaning of both the Hebrew and Greek words for soul and that it signified natural physical life. Armed with this information, her reading of Hebrews 4:12 suggested that the human soul and spirit were distinct substances which the Word of God was able to divide. The former died with the body, the latter "returned to God."

Hutchinson's question concerning the mortality of the soul sparked a lively exchange with several ministers, one in which she proved herself nearly as adept as they in marshaling scriptural quotations to defend her position. Her teacher John Cotton found her practically impervious to his arguments for the soul's immortality. Her idea that soul and body died and only the spirit returned to God seemed especially pernicious, undercutting traditional teaching that Jesus' death had redeemed both. When Cotton pointed this out, however, Hutchinson calmly replied that the Bible said nowhere that Jesus had come "to redeem the seed of Adam [the bodies of natural humanity] but the seed of Abraham," or the spirits of those who exercised true faith. When her pastor John Wilson asserted that God could transform an immortally miserable soul to make it "immortally happy," Hutchinson challenged him to show her this phrase from the Bible. When Wilson quoted St. Paul's prayer in I Thessalonians 5:23 that body, soul, and spirit be kept blameless "to Salvation," Hutchinson corrected him. It said that they are kept *"to the coming of Christ Jesus not to Salvation,"* she observed. This series of exchanges left no doubt that the woman at least knew her Bible and could draw on much of it from memory.

Ironically, Hutchinson was finally persuaded not by her teacher but by Governor John Winthrop and Reverend John

Davenport, the latter a relative newcomer to the colony. Winthrop found the first chink in Hutchinson's rhetorical armor with his observation that God's curse of death upon Adam in Genesis 3 did not imply annihilation of the soul and body, but only a separation of the two. Hutchinson promised to reflect upon Winthrop's remark, which she regarded as the most weighty idea yet spoken. Later in the exchange, Davenport explained that the curse on Adam condemned not the soul, but the *person* of Adam to die by rending soul from body. Hutchinson must learn to distinguish between the "*life of the Soule and the Life of the Body,*" Davenport explained. The body's life was mortal, but that of the soul immortal according to Ecclesiastes 12. Finally convinced, Hutchinson renounced her speculation about the soul's mortality. She admitted that she had misread the relevant passages: "*thear was my Mistake. I took Soule for Life.*"

The ministers' progress in persuading Hutchinson of the soul's immortality encouraged them to take on the related question of the resurrection of the body. For all parties, this issue turned on the question of whether, when a believer exercised true faith, her body as well as her soul became mystically "united to Christ Jesus." Hutchinson speculated that the believer's "death to sin" discussed in Romans 6:2–7 meant that the resurrection released the believer's soul from its present sinful body. It seemed repugnant to her that a holy Christ could be united to a physical body which was so polluted by the daily sins of human beings. She therefore speculated that at death, a believer's soul would enter a pure, newly created body. Yet this view contradicted traditional Christian teaching. The Bible taught that Christ redeemed the body as well as the soul, John Cotton explained. Both were "united to Christ." The raised body would be purified from sin and perfected to be holy and to obey.

Hutchinson could not declare herself convinced by Cotton's explanation, even after John Davenport weighed in with further elaboration. She began to waver only after Reverend Peter Bulkeley interrupted with a pointed question. Did she accept any concept of resurrection other than "Union to Christ Jesus?" If not, then did she hold "that foule, groce, filthye and abominable" Familist belief in the community of women? The two ideas were connected, the ministers explained. Familists thought that the Resurrection was merely a spiritual event which took place at conversion and had already happened for every true believer. But if the Resurrection lay in the past, the institution of marriage was also defunct. Jesus himself had said that in the Resurrection "they neither marry nor are given in marriage" (Matthew 22:30). Familists had reputedly concluded from this text that any union involving sexual relations between men and women came not through marriage "*but in a Way of Communitie.*" The ministers feared that Hutchinson's views would lead to the repudiation of marriage and the practice of free love.

Hutchinson recoiled from this implication, declaring that she would have to abandon her view if it led to such a conclusion. "*I abhor that Practice*" of Familist free love, she insisted. Yet her doubts about traditional views on the Resurrection persisted throughout the remainder of the first day's trial. She believed in a future resurrection, she said, confessing with St. Paul that without the Resurrection, "all is in vayne, both preaching and all" (I Corinthians 15:14). Yet she continued to maintain that "*the Body that dyes*" would not rise again. Believers would rise in Christ with a newly created body unconnected with the one which had died.

Hutchinson's refusal to be convinced on this point prompted the Boston church to move to an "Admonition," a solemn form of censure intended to warn its recipient to renounce erroneous belief or face excommunication. Its gravity prompted her oldest son Edward and son-in-law Thomas Savage, both of whom were present as church members, to object that she had not yet come to a firm position on the matter. They favored a delay that would give her time to think things over, but this only earned them a rebuke. The ministers chose John Cotton to deliver the Admonition, since Hutchinson respected his words more than any of theirs and might be more inclined to listen to him. As sunset darkened the meetinghouse, Anne Hutchinson's teacher took his stance before the exhausted woman.

This was a poignant moment for both. Hutchinson had crossed three thousand miles of ocean to for the privilege of sitting under the teaching of this man who had been driven from her by the ecclesiastical authorities in England. In Boston she had enjoyed his favor and encouragement in extending godly hospitality and ministering to the women of the community. Yet now she braced herself to bear up under words of censure from the teacher she had so much admired.

John Cotton retraced in his own memory the events since Hutchinson's arrival in the colony. He recalled how she had helped so many to gain a true understanding of God's grace. He praised her intelligence and talent, her helpfulness to her husband in governing their large family, and her keen perception, native eloquence, and ability to "express yourself in the Cause of God." Thomas Shepard fumed as Cotton recited the good she had done, perturbed that the Boston teacher seemed to be setting "a Crown . . . upon her Hed in the day of her Humiliation." Yet Cotton did not mince words in declaring that the evil of her opinions had outweighed "all the good of your doings." She had misled some into errors from which they might never recover. Indeed, the single error of denying the Resurrection of "thease very Bodies" struck a serious blow against the very foundation of faith. Cotton warned that her views on the Resurrection would not allow her to evade the Familist conclusion, opening the door to "promiscuous and filthie" sexual relations "without Distinction or Relation of Marriage."

Hutchinson's sense of shame appears to have grown heavier with each of Cotton's words, for she finally breached protocol by asking to speak. She apologized for the interruption, but feared that her weakness would make her forget what she wanted to say by the time Cotton had finished. After receiving permission, she declared that she had not held any of these beliefs " *before my Imprisonment.*"

Cotton conceded that he had not suspected her of holding such opinions until very recently and speculated that his own neglect had contributed to her fall into these dangerous ideas. Yet that did not diminish the severity of the damage her opinions had inflicted. He compared them to the rot of gangrene and the insidious spread of leprosy, threatening as they did to "eate out the very Bowells of Religion." They had so infected the Bay Colony churches, he lamented, that only God knew when they would be cured. Cotton concluded by admonishing Hutchinson to ask God for true repentance for her offense to God and the churches and to bewail her "weakness in the Sight of the Lord, that you may be pardoned."

The first day's trial finally ended at 8:00 p.m., but not before Thomas Shepard expressed his indignation that Hutchinson would interrupt her censure to "Impudently affirme" what he knew to be a lie. Hutchinson had earlier confided to him, he said, that she would have revealed even more of her aberrant beliefs than those reported at the trial if he had interviewed her before she was placed under house arrest. Most others, however, seemed satisfied with the progress they had made. John Winthrop recorded that everyone acknowledged "the special presence of God's spirit" in the proceedings, and the General Court licensed Hutchinson to lodge in Cotton's household while she waited for the continuation of her church trial the following Thursday. On balance, her conduct during the first day had persuaded the Court that there was some hope that she would repent.

During her week at Cotton's, Hutchinson engaged in extended discussions with her teacher and John Davenport, who had been a houseguest of Cotton's since his arrival the previous summer. The two ministers hoped that, by poring over the Bible with her, they could persuade her to renounce opinions which conflicted with Reformed Christianity and could secure the repentance which would restore her to fellowship with the Boston church. No direct record remains of their conversations, but Hutchinson must have relished many of the exchanges despite their purpose. She knew much of the Bible by heart. The chance to discuss its contents with two such learned ministers surely engaged her inquisitive mind as well as her taste for debate. Hutchinson's performance in both trials suggests that she was their intellectual equal, although Cotton and Davenport enjoyed the traditional male advantage of superior education in theology, biblical languages, and interpretation. The two ministers now brought all their training to bear upon the task of reducing Anne Hutchinson.

By the following Thursday, the two must have believed themselves close to success as they watched Hutchinson enter the Boston meetinghouse clutching a page of recantations written in her own hand. After elder Thomas Leverett finished reading a list of ten outstanding charges against her, Hutchinson lifted the page and began to read. She acknowledged that she had been deeply deceived in her views on the Resurrection. The opinion was very dangerous, she admitted. She better understood that Christ was united to a believer's body as well as spirit and that Jesus instilled created graces which enabled the believer to pursue a holy life. She acknowledged that the Ten Commandments remained a guide for the Christian life. She conceded the main point of the entire controversy—that sanctification could evidence justification—offering only two qualifications: sanctification had to flow from the grace Christ had given, not from human effort, and it needed the "witness of the Spirit," a God-given inner confidence that it was a genuine sign of grace. She even renounced the prophecy of doom which she had pronounced at her civil trial. She confessed that she had spoken rashly, "out of heate of Spirit and unadvisedly."

Hutchinson "acknowledged dayngerous error," "renounced" it, could "now see" better the truth of orthodox views, "confessed," and declared herself "hartely sorry" for impugning the ministers. She was saying all the right things to signal true repentance. Yet her public confession quickly began to unravel with a single remark which was not included in the written script. Under questioning, Hutchinson repeated her previous week's assertion that she had not adopted the errors listed on her sheet until after her conviction and house arrest in Roxbury. If Thomas Shepard believed otherwise, she declared, he was simply deceived.

Shepard bristled at this fateful remark. Mrs. Hutchinson should be filled with "Shame and Confusion" for the errors she was admitting, he retorted. Instead, she was trying to shift shame onto Shepard by saying he was mistaken. Moreover, her confession minimized her "groce Errors" by terming them mere mistakes. Shepard thought such statements inconsistent with true repentance. The Roxbury minister John Eliot concurred, observing that Hutchinson had confided to him as well as Shepard many suspect beliefs which she had held *before* her imprisonment.

Even John Cotton could not swallow Hutchinson's claim to have held none of these views before her conviction, nor could many of the Boston church members who had gathered to listen to her confession. Hoping to elicit a confession of at least her most well-known view, Cotton asked whether she had not previously held that there were "*no distinct graces inherent in us but all was in Christ Jesus?*" Indeed, this troublesome idea had formed the nub of the controversy. Her denial that believers possessed in themselves such graces as love and peace implied that there was no need for ministers who could teach them to cultivate these virtues, no need for magistrates or laws to restrain the remnants of sin. Believers could throw off all constraints, opening the door to Muenster-like chaos and anarchy.

Here was Hutchinson's chance to demonstrate the depth and sincerity of her repentance. Well before her conviction, most members of the Boston church had heard her deny inherent graces in unmistakable terms. Yet she flatly refused to admit what everyone in the meetinghouse regarded as the moral failing of embracing serious doctrinal error. A simple mistake was much more palatable to her, and she would acknowledge nothing more. "*I did mistake the word Inherent,*" she insisted.

Consternation swept across the congregation. Too many had heard her pronouncements on this point during the past two years to believe that they had been mere mistakes. An indignant Thomas Shepard voiced what everyone present already knew: Hutchinson had not only denied the *word* "inherent," she had denied the very concept itself. In her weekly meetings and private spiritual counsel with many women, she had habitually denied the existence of what the godly termed "creature graces"—divine instillation into a believer's heart of such virtues as patience or faith.

Hutchinson had made a fatal error, one she only compounded when she followed up to insist that "My Judgment is not altered though my Expression alters." The claim precipitated a deluge of rebuttals. John Wilson warned that even if he conceded her point, expressions which apparently denied creature graces still contradicted the truth. Zechariah Symmes declared that her denial of inherent grace was not new; she had held this for a long time. Deputy Governor Thomas Dudley remarked sarcastically that her repentance was "*in a paper*" but unobservable "*on her countenance.*" He wondered darkly whether she had truly written her confession herself, implying that Cotton and Davenport may have coached her. Thomas Weld recalled that when he had spoken with her of graces long before, Hutchinson had told him she would not pray such graces as faith and patience. Her refusal implied that she did not need to do so; she was a mere channel for the grace of Christ himself. Several of the women whom Hutchinson had counseled about this very issue, now disillusioned by her denial, later confided to John Winthrop that they would also have testified against her "if their modesty had not restrained them."

Hutchinson's denial had undone the credibility of her entire written confession. Reverend John Eliot observed that anyone using her attempted distinction between a mistake and an error might easily dispense with every retraction she had written, hiding their true convictions beneath a sheet of clever words. She had asserted a manifest untruth, fueling a deep suspicion that her confession was a sham. By clinging to her claim in the face of overwhelming contrary testimony, Hutchinson only confirmed the assembly's misgivings.

Hutchinson's recalcitrance prompted the ministers to advocate her immediate excommunication. In Hugh Peter's view, the magnitude of her offense required a much fuller repentance than she had offered. To him, such errors revealed that Hutchinson had never learned the basic teachings of her catechism. The rebuke surely stung this godly minister's daughter who had served nearly three years as John Cotton's virtual teaching assistant among the women of the Boston church. Peter also charged that Hutchinson had stepped out of her place, "*you have rather bine a Husband than a Wife and a Preacher than a Hearer; and a Magistrate than a Subject.*" Thomas Shepard regarded her as unqualified for church membership in the first place. To him, Hutchinson's refusal to confess her "horrible Untruths" indicated that she never had any true grace in her heart, but was a "Notorious Imposter." The charge certainly stung this woman who had been supremely confident of her own salvation. Even John Cotton, who had invested so much of his time and reputation to rescue the gifted woman he had long regarded his "deare friend," finally gave up on her. He mused that he saw no alternative in this circumstance but to invoke the declaration of Revelation 22:15. Since she had maintained a lie, she must be thrown out of the church to join "dogs and such as love and make lyes." He therefore deferred to his colleague John Wilson, whose job it was as pastor to administer church discipline when a "Lye is open and persisted in."

Hugh Peter's charge that Hutchinson had been rather "a husband than a wife, a preacher than a hearer, a magistrate than a subject" constitutes the most succinct summary of Anne Hutchinson's unfeminine behavior. Many historians have cited this statement in support of the view that gender somehow lay at the heart of the entire controversy. This observation is undeniable, yet Peter's words appear in this particular context as examples of the broader charges of duplicity and fraudulence which Cotton cited as the true reason for her excommunication. To be sure, John Winthrop believed that Hutchinson had usurped her husband William, whom he thought "wholly ruled" by her. She appeared to adopt a preaching role in the leadership of her weekly meetings, but the legal force of Peter's charge depended on Winthrop's failed argument during her civil trial that her meetings had been public. The charge that she had usurped the magistracy is more obscure, although the historian Mary Beth Norton has argued that this charge hinted at a subtle but threatening violation of the seventeenth-century assumption that fathers of a certain rank should wield political power while mothers—even those of high rank such as Hutchinson—should simply obey the civil law, confining their influence to social spheres outside the realm of political power. The free grace faction of which Hutchinson was a part certainly did pose a political challenge to colonial leadership, though as we have seen, it did so directly through the actions of Hutchinson's male associates such as Sir Henry Vane and her brother-in-law John Wheelwright. Hutchinson herself denied any intention to "cross a rule" which restricted women's role even in religious affairs, let alone in matters of colonial government.

Hutchinson had fallen silent sometime before and remained so until the final moments of the trial. To John Winthrop she appeared "somewhat dejected" as the members of the Boston church debated briefly whether to excommunicate or to give her a second admonition. John Cotton argued that the church should treat her as the New Testament character Ananias, who had lied flagrantly to his church and had been immediately cast out. The Boston church then voted to excommunicate Hutchinson for stating and defending a lie before God and her congregation, and for aggravating the offense by doing so on a day set aside for her to confess and repent. In pronouncing the sentence, Pastor John Wilson also cited her for disturbing the Church and seducing "many a poor soule" with her erroneous beliefs. "*I do cast you out*," he intoned, "and in the name of Christ *I do deliver you up to Sathan* that you may learne no more to blaspheme to seduce and to lye."

As Wilson's words faded to silence, John Winthrop noted that Hutchinson's spirits visibly brightened, and she "gloried in her sufferings, saying, that it was the greatest happiness, next to Christ, that ever befell her." Yet despite her brave face and defiant words, the trial's outcome marked the death of her position in the church and community. Her longsuffering teacher had abandoned her. Men she had cherished as "brothers in the Lord" had voted to excommunicate her. Women whom she had given spiritual counsel now avoided her gaze. She left the meetinghouse stripped of her good name as a leading godly gentlewoman who had been an "Instrument of doing some good amongst us."

With the conclusion of her church trial Anne Hutchinson's sojourn in Massachusetts Bay reached its end. Winthrop waited no more than three days before sending a warrant ordering Hutchinson to leave Massachusetts before the last day of March and releasing her from house arrest so that she could begin packing. Her husband William had already begun preparations to leave the colony. Indeed, during Hutchinson's church trial he and several companions were scouting a good site for a new home in the region of Narragansett Bay. The group first petitioned authorities at Plymouth for permission to settle there. The magistrates at Plymouth had been following events in Boston, however, and they refused the fractious settlers permission to settle in the colony. They would allow them only to negotiate with the Narragansetts for land outside Plymouth's borders. The group selected Aquidneck Island, later renamed Rhode Island, and prepared to establish a new settlement there.

On March 28, 1638, Anne Hutchinson turned her back on Boston and stepped into the final phase of her life. She journeyed

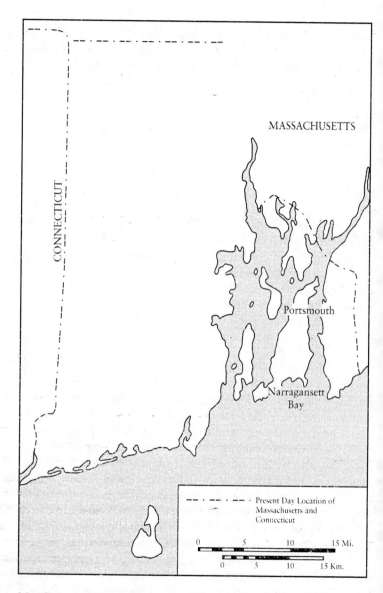

Map 7-1 Aquidneck/Rhode Island Region.

first to the family farm in Mount Wollaston. There she expected to meet John Wheelwright's wife and family, who were also packing to leave for Pascataquack (soon renamed Exeter) in New Hampshire. Wheelwright himself was already in New Hampshire, having decided against a new settlement with the Hutchinsons because of the taint of heresy attached to them. John Winthrop had heard that Hutchinson initially planned to sail with her sister-in-law to New Hampshire. At "the Mount," however, Mary Wheelwright may have told her that her views would not be welcome in Pascataquack. Hutchinson may also have learned that her husband had made sufficient progress on their home site for her to join him immediately. Whatever the reason, Hutchinson changed course and set off cross country to reunite with her husband and family on Aquidneck Island in Narragansett Bay.

Nearly everything known about Hutchinson's final years comes from a few entries scattered through the middle pages of John Winthrop's journal. Winthrop's conviction that Hutchinson was a very dangerous woman led him to focus on reports of tumult, faction, and extravagant behavior in her new Rhode Island home. Even so, glimpses of the Hutchinson family's efforts to regroup show through.

Several of the Hutchinson family's closest friends and supporters joined them on Aquidneck Island. Before they left Boston, William Coddington, William Aspinwall, John Coggeshall, and William Hutchinson joined with fifteen other men to sign a town covenant for their new home in Portsmouth at the northwest end of the island. The decision to follow Bay Colony precedent in signing a covenant, as well as the contents of the covenant itself, demonstrate that neither Hutchinson's family nor those of the other signatories were the sort of libertine Antinomians their Bostonian detractors had feared. Neither were they champions of liberty of conscience in the stamp of Roger Williams, who had preceded them to Narragansett Bay.

The Portsmouth covenant suggests the kind of regime at least some of Anne Hutchinson's supporters may have attempted to institute had the free grace faction won the contest of influence in Massachusetts Bay. Far from creating a more free and tolerant society, the initial blueprint for Portsmouth bore far more resemblance to a theocratic despotism—a dictatorship ruled by divine law—than to the chartered colony of English freeholders from which they had recently come. The founding document solemnly bound its signers to "incorporate our selves into a Bodie Politick" to which each signer would "submit our persons, lives, and estates unto our Lord Jesus Christ . . . and to all those perfect and most absolute laws of his given us in his holy words of truth, to be guided and Judged thereby." They chose John Coddington, who had once served as local magistrate and a Boston deputy to the General Court, to serve as "Judge" after the pattern of Old Testament rulers of that title. Coddington may have intended to hold the position only temporarily until the hoped-for return of Sir Henry Vane to New England. When Vane did not show up at Aquidneck Island, however, this attempt at divine rule through a prophetic agent of God quickly broke down.

Hutchinson herself soon became a spiritual leader of the fledgling town of Portsmouth. In fact, John Winthrop regarded her as the real power behind whatever civil leadership her husband William exerted there. Whatever truth lay in Winthrop's jaundiced assessment of William as "wholly guided by his wife," she continued to loom large in the Massachusetts governor's early entries concerning Portsmouth.

In her early months at Portsmouth, however, Hutchinson endured a difficult pregnancy which kept her inactive during the summer of 1638. Indeed, by early August her "distempered" body and flagging spirits made her fear she was about to die. She summoned the Aquidneck physician and preacher John Clarke, who attended her premature delivery of what Winthrop termed a "monstrous birth." Modern physicians have identified the delivery as a "hydatidiform mole," an abnormal pregnancy in which a sperm duplicates its own DNA after fertilizing an empty egg, producing an unformed or partially formed mass of tissue. In Hutchinson's case, Dr. Clarke counted "twenty-six or twenty-seven" distinct lumps which he examined and described with meticulous care. The defect has always been recognized as a risk in women over forty; even today it occurs about once in every thousand pregnancies. In the context of seventeenth-century belief about such matters, it constituted yet another blow to Hutchinson's already shattered reputation.

Hutchinson's adversaries in Boston did not hesitate to draw an ominous moral from her misfortune. John Cotton was the first to learn of the event in a letter from Hutchinson's husband William. Unlike his discreet treatment of Mary Dyer's case the previous year, Cotton announced Anne Hutchinson's monstrous birth from the pulpit the Sunday after he learned of it. He speculated to the congregation that the incident was divine punishment for her "error in denying inherent righteousness," the belief about which Hutchinson had lied during her church trial the previous March. Reverend Thomas Weld saw Hutchinson's and Mary Dyer's monstrous births as dual examples of God's judgment on their wayward beliefs. In Weld's view, God had adapted his judgment to Hutchinson's sin in every detail. She had vented "misshapen opinions, so she must bring forth deformed monsters."

Hutchinson would soon have heard through friends and family in Boston of how Cotton had turned her misfortune into an object lesson on the consequences of doctrinal error. The news no doubt contributed to her outburst of bitterness against the Boston church. It may also have constituted one of several issues which prompted her to compose a written "admonition" which she sent to the Boston church in March, 1639. The elders refused to read it publicly because Hutchinson had been excommunicated. It has since been lost. The last recorded effort at official contact between Anne Hutchinson and members from her former church occurred when the delegation from Boston visited a year later in March 1640, only to have her greet them with suspicion and denounce their church as a "Whore and Strumpet."

Hutchinson's excommunication and departure from Boston appears to have set her on a course of spiritual exploration and speculation during the final years of her life. As often happens among dissenting factions, the founders of Portsmouth soon discovered disagreements among themselves. Hostile reports filtered to Winthrop of "one Nicholas Easton" at Portsmouth who taught that the Holy Ghost and the devil indwelt believers simultaneously, and "one Herne," who declared that women did not possess souls. Hutchinson herself continued to seek direct manifestations of the Spirit's presence. Winthrop learned of one instance when a minor earthquake shook a house in which Hutchinson and some friends were at prayer. According to the report he received, Hutchinson insisted that the Holy Ghost was the one shaking the house while descending upon those gathered in prayer, just as the Spirit had done upon the New Testament apostles. This potpourri of religious expression eventually led to division as John Coddington led a number of exiles to the southern end of Aquidneck Island, where he founded Newport.

Hutchinson's late religious views may best be described as "Seeker," if she was indeed responsible for the ideas expressed by the handful of people John Winthrop identified as her followers. Two of these, her son Francis and son-in-law William Collins, were arrested while visiting Boston in the fall of 1641 for a letter Collins had written charging that all Massachusetts churches and ministers were "antichristian." They justified this assertion by claiming that the church had ceased to exist after New Testament times, so the ordination of ministers was no longer legitimate. This idea bore strong resemblance to the central Seeker tenet eventually advocated by Rhode Island's Roger Williams, among others, that the true church had vanished from the earth only a generation after the apostles died. True believers must now wait and seek for God's restoration of the church with apostolic power. This appears consistent with the surviving fragments of information concerning Hutchinson's own religious practice, including her refusal to recognize the legitimacy of church authority and her quest for direct encounter with the Holy Spirit.

Alongside Hutchinson's ongoing spiritual pursuits, the surviving evidence suggests that she and William managed to reconstruct a family life during their years in Portsmouth. Several children remained in the Hutchinson household at the time of their exile from Boston, and these traveled with them to their new home in Portsmouth. Anne and William celebrated the marriage of their daughter Anne to William Collins in 1639 or 1640. Their son Edward and daughter Faith came to Portsmouth for a short time in 1638 along with Faith's husband Thomas Savage. All three soon returned to Boston, where they remained members of the church despite their mother's views. They continued to keep in touch by correspondence and visits between Portsmouth and Boston. William probably kept his share of the partnership in the Boston wharf and may have relied on Edward to represent his interest with other shareholders. The second son Richard ended up in London, probably to work with relatives there.

The presence of extended family members in Old England and New enabled the Hutchinsons to strengthen their transatlantic mercantile activities and to expand to Barbados.

In 1642, Hutchinson's devoted husband William died. Shortly after his death, she with her grown son Francis, her daughter Anne, and her son-in-law William Collins decided to take the five children still living in her household to neighboring Dutch New Netherlands. Massachusetts authorities had been working to bring Narragansett Bay and Aquidneck Island under their own jurisdiction, a possibility Hutchinson wanted to avoid at all costs. There they established what she termed her "city of refuge" with a few other families on Pelham Bay in Long Island Sound (the site is now in the northwest corner of Pelham Bay Park in the Bronx). Her daughter Anne and son-in-law William Collins also went with her. The early months on Pelham Bay must have gone relatively well, for John Winthrop records that they had established cooperative relations with the local native Wecqueasgeek people. Before long, however, longstanding tensions between the Wecqueasgeeks and the Dutch exploded into open warfare, sweeping Hutchinson's fledgling settlement into its wake.

In the late summer of 1643, a band of Wecqueasgeek warriors appeared at Hutchinson's door as if to pay a neighborly visit. Before the family could react, their visitors struck. The warriors killed Hutchinson and "Mr. Collins, her son-in-law" along with all her family except eight-year-old Susanna, whom they captured and adopted into the tribe. Several members of the two neighboring English families also died in the attack. A few escaped to tell the tale. Within months, the news spread to England, where Hutchinson's old enemy Reverend Thomas Weld was putting the finishing touches on his preface to Winthrop's *Short Story* of the so-called Antinomian crisis. He could not confirm the exact manner of her death, Weld wrote, "but slaine it seems she is, according to all reports." To him, the news seemed a fitting conclusion to his account of what had transpired in Massachusetts six years before. The hand of divine Providence had selected "this wofull woman, to make her and those belonging to her" a stark example of Wecqueasgeek cruelty.

"The Sainted Anne Hutchinson"

Thomas Weld's concluding assessment of Anne Hutchinson as a "great and sore affliction" on the colonists of Massachusetts Bay was far from the last word concerning her, even in her own generation. Within a few months after the appearance of John Winthrop's *Short Story of the Rise, Reign and Ruin of the Antinomians, Familists, and Libertines*, John Wheelwright and others of Hutchinson's friends and family read the account and determined to set the record straight. In 1645, the result of this effort appeared in London as *Mercurius Americanus,* a pamphlet written primarily to vindicate Wheelwright himself of the charges of error and sedition included in Weld's preface to the *Short Story.*

Mercurius mentioned Hutchinson only briefly, in part to challenge Weld's characterization of her as the primary leader of the free grace faction. In *Mercurius* she appeared as "the first among women," yet only one of many whose appetite for unorthodox ideas would never have gone so far had the General Court's aggressive prosecution "forced them into a habit." The Anne Hutchinson of *Mercurius Americanus* was not only a woman of "good wit" but "naturally of a good judgment too," a fact *Mercurius* thought readily observable in the various social functions she performed as one of Boston's leading gentlewomen. To be sure, *Mercurius* acknowledged that in her spiritual life she was too readily influenced by the power of suggestion and immediate, internal impulses. As a result, the author admitted that she experienced "many strange fancies, and erroneous tenets possess her." The author noted that she was especially susceptible to such fancies during her confinement toward the end of her pregnancies when she also experienced "melancholy"—an affliction twenty-first century psychologists might call depression. Nevertheless, *Mercurius* depicted her not as a ringleader but a victim of the prosecutorial zeal of Winthrop and the General Court, who refused to take her infirmities or melancholy into account when they unjustly decided to expel her from Massachusetts Bay Colony.

Few who have written about Anne Hutchinson in the centuries since her death have accepted *Mercurius's* denial that she had ever been "Captain" of an Antinomian faction in early New England. Most have adopted the *Short Story's* depiction of Hutchinson as the leader of the Antinomians in Massachusetts, even if they prefer to see her as a martyr rather than a villain. She has been portrayed alternately as a visionary prophet of freedom of conscience or as the misguided leader of an insurgent faction; as the victim of either her own overreaching ambition or the oppression of a monolithic Puritan "orthodoxy;" as an imaginative woman who could not distinguish the voice of God from her own menopausal delusions or as a courageous woman who challenged the gender norms of her day. Only in the first years of the twenty-first century has the historian Michael Winship offered an interpretation which has taken seriously the claims of *Mercurius,* shifting much responsibility for the controversy to male advocates of free grace such as Sir Henry Vane and to zealous heresy-hunting sanctificationists such as Thomas Shepard.

It is not difficult to see elements of all of these depictions in the story of her life, but who was the real Anne Hutchinson, as she understood herself? What does her story tell us about her own time and place, and how does it fit into the American story? The answers to such questions are difficult to extract from the layers of conflicting interpretation which have built up in the centuries since Thomas Shepard first wrote John Cotton of his concern about "quarrels secretly begun" in late spring 1636. Nearly every surviving piece of evidence about Hutchinson's life has been filtered through the lens of the free grace controversy. Even her own surviving words have been shaped by the verbal thrust and parry of formal trials in courtroom and church. She selected most of her words very carefully to defend herself or counter her prosecutors, to guard her true thoughts from hostile accusers who were prepared to use every stray word against her. Her outbursts were part of that adversarial context as well. As such, they too have the potential to mislead. Perhaps they represent an unguarded window into her true beliefs. Yet they may just as readily have been what she claimed—rash, ill-considered expressions which she might never have stated or seriously entertained if not provoked and exhausted by hours of relentless, hostile questioning.

The surviving evidence of her life permits only a suggestive sketch of the real Anne Hutchinson, not the detailed portrait we would so much like to have. Yet by setting her within her seventeenth-century context of militant English Protestantism, we can catch a glimpse of a woman of superior intellectual gifts who was devoted to employing them in all of the ways her puritan family, friends, and teachers encouraged her to do. She would probably never have achieved such influence in early Massachusetts had she not been a model of godly womanhood. She ministered tirelessly to her neighbors in many practical demonstrations of hospitality, care for the sick, assistance in childbirth, and spiritual counsel. She managed all of this while partnering with her husband William in raising a large family, a responsibility which she apparently carried out very well.

Indeed, at her church trial John Cotton singled out for special compliment her contribution to the "government" of the Hutchinson family. The subsequent careers of several surviving children suggest her and William's skill in this supremely important area of puritan life. The children's ability to survive this tragic chain of events and to thrive and prosper as one of New England's leading merchant families hints at the strength of the bond between William and Anne. They also speak well of William's own acumen, despite John Winthrop's dismissal of him as a man "wholly governed by his wife." The few glimpses the record affords of their marriage suggest a couple devoted to one another. William does not appear in the record of either of Anne's trials, but this does not mean he had withdrawn his support from her. He told the Boston church emissaries to Portsmouth in 1640 that he regarded her "a dear saint and servant of God," and there is no reason to believe that this reflected any recent change of opinion. In fact, he was not present at her church trial in March 1638 because he was performing the duties of a devoted husband and father, preparing a future on Aquidneck Island for his exiled family. There he applied the remaining years of his life to securing and extending his family's fortunes, working together with other exiles such as John Coggeshall to establish a merchant community which would shape the future of Rhode Island as a center of Atlantic commerce. When he died, he left to his children a strong family mercantile network that extended throughout the English Atlantic world.

Anne and William Hutchinson's children carried on this legacy of business and community leadership. Their eldest son Edward remained a member of the Boston church throughout his life and became a pillar of the community, an important merchant, a land speculator, and a military officer. Their daughter Faith married Thomas Savage and helped establish another of the Bay Colony's leading family lines before her death in Boston in 1652. Their youngest daughter, Susanna, carried off by the Wecqueasgeeks at the time of her mother's murder, was returned to Boston four years later and eventually married John Cole, with whom she raised a family of seven children. Their son Richard returned to London, where he helped to anchor a transatlantic family mercantile interest that endured into the eighteenth century and kept the family near the center of Massachusetts' political life for generations. Indeed, Anne Hutchinson's great-great grandson Thomas became the Lieutenant Governor of the colony during the run-up to the American Revolution. His role in carrying out British policy during that conflict earned him the hatred of Patriot leaders, and he recapitulated his famous ancestor's exile in 1774, 136 years after Anne Hutchinson said goodbye to Boston.

Anne Hutchinson's powerful intellect enabled her to parlay the respect earned from her success as a model mother into a role of spiritual leadership within the Boston church. She possessed an intuitive ability to take the learning available to women of her own day and apply it to search meaning out of the text of Scripture for herself, as her beloved teacher John Cotton taught her to do. She exhibited a passion for truth, especially where assurance of salvation was concerned—a determination to get that doctrine right for herself and a zeal for spreading it to her friends and associates in the community. It seems unnecessary to trace the ideas of such an intelligent and resourceful woman back to an English Puritan underground, as some historians have done. Any such connections can be no more than speculative, given the surviving evidence. Hutchinson certainly had the intellectual and interpretive tools she needed to select certain ideas on free grace from Cotton's and Wheelwright's sermons and to develop them further into a theology distinctly her own.

Like most other godly women of her day, Anne Hutchinson was determined to hew to the rule of Scripture as she understood it, remaining within the boundaries she believed God had ordained for her sex. Yet she also threw her energy into making the most of every opportunity she discovered within her sphere, especially in her role as a godly gentlewoman within a heady experimental religious environment far from the constraints of Archbishop Laud's Church of England. Thus, she conducted all her activities precisely as a godly gentlewoman, despite Hugh Peter's charge that she "had rather bine a Husband than a wife." She helped women in childbirth to find assurance that they would reach heaven if they died during delivery. She gave them confidence that their children might eventually find that assurance too. She extended hospitality to godly families newly arrived from England. She quenched gossip concerning her aloofness by welcoming the godly into her home to discuss the ministers' sermons, a practice common among Puritan women.

The aspect of Hutchinson's identity which ultimately proved her undoing was her claim to prophetic gifts. She coupled this with an inflexible certainty about the moral rightness of her views which tends to characterize most who believe themselves prophets. At her church trial, to be sure, she confessed that she had pronounced "rashly and out of heate of Spirit and unadvisedly" the prophecy of doom against Massachusetts which had gotten her banished from the colony. Yet she never renounced her belief that she could hear the voice of God's Spirit speaking through the words of Scripture directly to her soul. Nor could she bring herself to renounce the rightness of her conclusions in the things which mattered most to her. At the crucial moment in her church trial, she could not bring herself to confess moral error in her denial of "inherent graces" in believers, even though doing so would have saved her from excommunication. She insisted that she had made a mere "mistake," reducing what she had said on this matter to the level of a misstatement, not the dangerous error which even John Cotton and many of her followers testified that she had purveyed. When she left the meetinghouse after her excommunication, she reiterated her moral rightness by declaring it "better to be cast out of the Church then to deny Christ."

The fragmentary evidence of Hutchinson's final years suggests that she remained inflexibly bound to her own theological views to the day she died. Her participation in the attempt to find a theocracy in Portsmouth suggests he was certainly no champion of the liberty of conscience and religious toleration. Her role in the fractiousness which divided the Portsmouth colony within two years does little to redeem her, nor does her apparent inability to coexist with others who did not share her convictions.

Even with Hutchinson's peculiarities, however, it is difficult to escape the suggestion of *Mercurius Americanus* that if Bay Colony leaders had not acted as *"persecuting Prelates,"* her story might have turned out differently. During the early years of Massachusetts Bay, John Winthrop's practice of "covering with love" many errors and lapses of the colonists had helped to facilitate harmonious relations amid the welter and ferment of differing theological views which multiplied with the arrival of each new ship from England. Perhaps it was the zealous prosecution of men such as Winthrop, Thomas Dudley, and Thomas Shepard which forced Hutchinson's minor taste for theological novelty into a fatal habit which precipitated her downfall. Perhaps Hutchinson and other adherents of free grace would never have formed a faction, if only Winthrop had maintained his covering of love. Perhaps Hutchinson would have moderated her theological views and remained a "profitable member" in Boston society to the natural end of her life, if only the authorities had followed *Mercurius's* prescription to pursue a more moderate disposition toward their brothers and sisters in faith. Perhaps Hutchinson would never have escalated her own moderate revelations into an attack on the colonial ministers, if only firebrands such as Sir Henry Vane had not egged her on. If so, she might have passed into obscurity with little trace of her life, no story of an iconic woman standing defiant before a bench of stern, black-clad persecutors.

Mercurius reminds us that, even for some of Anne Hutchinson's contemporaries, it was possible to imagine a different outcome to her story, one in which the Puritans of Massachusetts Bay continued to cover with love Hutchinson's energetic leadership of the women's community in Boston. The early chapters of her narrative illuminate the possibilities which seventeenth-century Puritanism opened to women, as well as the constraints of gender which persisted in Puritan circles. Indeed, the end game of Hutchinson's civil trial—her prophecy concerning the destruction of the Massachusetts General Court—turns out to have been practically the only time she unambiguously crossed the gender line. To be sure, her earlier activities—including her brilliant defense at her trial—may have pressed against the limits of puritan gender norms. Even so, members of the General Court ultimately had to concede her activities as a leader of Boston's free grace faction had not explicitly transgressed women's bounds.

The boundaries of theology, however, were another matter. Here Hutchinson's church trial demonstrated that the direction she took in her own development of John Cotton's teaching eventually did carry her into unorthodox theological territory. Indeed, her idiosyncratic reading of New Testament texts led her to deny certain basic tenets of ancient creeds which Christians had confessed for over a thousand years. Rumors of her theological transgressions eventually attracted the attention of the heresy-hunting Thomas Shepard. Shepard then traced imaginative links to groups such as the Familists whose presence in England—which had never been strong—had waned decades before. The lurking anxiety that colonists might be seduced into deviant theology was certainly fanned into fury by suspicion that an influential woman was spreading aberrant views. If the specter of Familism aroused fears of social anarchy, a woman at the head of a suspected Familist cell would only serve as a living embodiment of the imagined threat. Yet it was not the leadership of a woman in itself, but Hutchinson's putative link with Familism, which triggered alarm. Before Massachusetts authorities drew that link, Hutchinson's leadership in the community of early Boston was almost universally welcomed and encouraged.

The author of *Mercurius Americanus* was a perceptive student of human nature. History is filled with examples of overzealous prosecutors whose penchant for connecting imaginary dots pushes their targets into circling the wagons around what were initially innocent or naive mistakes. In 1637, such a dynamic ripped Massachusetts Bay in two, inflicting wounds in the community and its people which took decades to heal. In the process, it sent a woman of "good wit" and "excellent judgment" into exile and eventual violent death, along with too many of her children.

It is one of history's ironies that this seventeenth-century tragedy has produced an enduring American icon—ironic, but not surprising. Anne Hutchinson's story is too deliciously archetypical. It contains all the elements needed to fashion an enduring origins myth capable of mirroring the anxieties and aspirations of successive generations of Americans. The lone individual standing for principle against a phalanx of oppressors has formed one of the country's most compelling motifs—a story Americans have told themselves about themselves time and again since the American Revolution. Religious dissenters have told this story even longer. Indeed, Anne Hutchinson's contemporary, Roger Williams, has occupied a distinguished place as one of its earliest embodiments—an apostle of Toleration and Liberty of Conscience.

Anne Hutchinson's gender, however, has complicated her place in this story of rising American individualism by invoking another more threatening image—that of Eve's fall and seduction of her husband, resulting in the entry of sin, disorder, and moral chaos into the world. This association lay very close to the surface of Hugh Peter's complaint that Hutchinson had usurped the role of a husband, and of John Cotton's warning that her beliefs would lead to "promiscuous and filthie" sexual relations. It informed the eighteenth-century portrayal of Hutchinson as a potential New England John of Leyden bent on destroying the colony in Antinomian fire and blood. It prevented nineteenth-century historians such as Charles Francis Adams from making a hero of Anne Hutchinson as they tended to do with Roger Williams. To be sure, the Massachusetts General Court and clergy played the role of narrow-minded persecutors in both accounts. Yet where Adams and others could see Williams as a "type of the advanced thinkers of his time," they could only see Hutchinson as a reckless fanatic who endangered the early Bay Colony's survival. Similarly, Nathaniel Hawthorne's fictional Anne Hutchinson, Hester Prynne, posed a troubling threat so long as she remained in the grip of radical, individual prophetic delusion. Only by relinquishing such pretentions for a life of disinterested benevolence could the woman render herself truly "sainted," not merely harmless, but a positive benefit to the community. The early twentieth-century statue of Hutchinson on the Massachusetts statehouse lawn betrays the same impulse to tame her memory, portraying her as a mother with arm cast protectively across the figure of a young girl who clings to her skirts.

Anne Hutchinson remains a potent icon. The virago of Thomas Weld's and John Winthrop's *Short Story* has come to be remembered more sympathetically, but not as the mere victim of "persecuting prelates" which *Mercurius Americanus* described. This side of her story has certainly not disappeared, forming as it does a feature of a persistent but ultimately unpersuasive narrative of Anne Hutchinson as a martyr for religious toleration and liberty of conscience. But the most recent interest in her life has focused more on her role of transgressor than martyr. Analysis of her transgressions has helped to illuminate the social boundaries of women's experience in the seventeenth century, in word as well as in deed, in theology as well as in social life. It has helped historians to understand Massachusetts during the Great Migration as a place where many of those boundaries were less fixed, more fluid, and far more open to debate and negotiation than earlier generations of historians had imagined they could have been.

Even so, the recent attention to Hutchinson as an icon of transgression may not differ so much from the uses previous generations have made of her story. Current interpretations may tell us as much about our own hopes and fears they do about Hutchinson in her time. We twenty-first century Americans are nothing if not alert to the dynamics of choice, constraint, oppression, and resistance. This sensitivity has introduced new insights—and perhaps, new distortions yet unrecognized—into Hutchinson's story. More than 375 years after she went into exile, the story of the "sainted Anne Hutchinson" is still being remembered and revised. Americans may never tire of retelling a story so potent as hers.

Glossary of Terms

adiaphora: a Greek term meaning "matters indifferent," which was applied to ceremonies and forms of worship required by the English Book of Common Prayer but not prescribed in the Bible. Defenders of the Prayer Book insisted that the forms did no harm to a person's faith and helped to preserve order and uniformity in English worship. Detractors argued that if the forms were truly indifferent—not prescribed by the Bible—they could be omitted without harm.

Anabaptists: literally "rebaptizers," these radical reformers believed that only true believers who could exercise their own faith should receive the rite of baptism. They rebaptized any who had been baptized in infancy and refused to baptize their own children until those children exercised individual faith. See also "baptism."

antinomian: a term derived from Greek literally meaning "against (anti) law (nomos)." Widely regarded as heretical by English Protestant leaders, antinomians were thought to believe that true faith in Jesus released the believer from obligation to observe the moral law expressed in the Ten Commandments of the Old Testament. Protestants used this term to describe many different beliefs. One of the most common in Anne Hutchinson's day was the idea that when people believed, God's Holy Spirit so overwhelmed their will that they no longer wanted to sin.

assurance: an inner sense of confidence that one has truly believed, been justified or made right with God, and possesses the promise of eternal life.

baptism: a rite of initiation into the Christian faith. In early modern England it was usually administered to infants of Christian parents shortly after birth by sprinkling or pouring water on the head, or by dipping the infant in water. Unbaptized adults received the rite at conversion. Protestants named baptism as one of two "sacraments." See also "sacrament."

Baptist: similar to Anabaptists (see above), Baptists taught that only those exercising active faith should receive the rite of baptism. See also "baptism."

bishop: an officer in the Episcopal form of church government who was appointed over a territory or diocese made up of many different churches. Bishops held power to rule church affairs and appoint priests and other church officials within their dioceses.

Book of Common Prayer: often referred to simply as the "prayer book," this book contained the official prayers, recitations, readings, forms of worship, church calendar, and summary of doctrine for the Church of England. In theory, every parish church was required to follow the forms and use the prayers contained in this book.

Calvin, John (1509–1564): a leading French Protestant Reformer. Calvin stressed the absolute sovereignty of God over all things and the concept of "predestination" (see below). He was known for his insistence that church doctrine and practice be governed by strict adherence to the teachings of the Bible.

Calvinism: a set of Protestant beliefs attributed to the Reformer John Calvin, which included a stress on the sovereignty of God, the doctrine of predestination, and the Bible as the sole source of truth about God, salvation, and Christian practice.

church covenant: in Congregational churches, an agreement among all members of the church to support one another in faith, to obey their leaders, to live according to the teachings of the Bible, and to hold each other accountable to those teachings. Congregationalists believed that God was a solemn witness to every person's agreement to such a covenant, blessed those who remained faithful to it, and punished those who violated it.

clergy: the body or collection of official priests or ministers of a church.

cleric: any particular priest or minister of a church.

Communion: see "Lord's Supper."

community of women: a belief attributed to Familists that true faith and union with Christ abolished the need for marriage among believing men and women, opening the door to a sixteenth-century form of free love. See "Familists."

conformer, conformity: a minister or layperson who observed the prescribed ceremonies, forms of worship, and regulations of the Church of England.

congregational: a type of church government in which the members of each individual local church assumed sole responsibility for its own affairs, including the election of all officers and the appointment of all ministers. Congregational churches acknowledged no formal responsibility to any ecclesiastical governing authority outside the local church.

conventicle: a private gathering for Bible reading, prayer, and religious discussion outside of regularly scheduled times of worship. The groups might include clergy as well as laypeople and often met in private homes or secluded locations. In England they were considered subversive and were outlawed.

conversion: the process of becoming a true believer. In Reformed thought this was God's doing and happened instantaneously when an elect person—one chosen by God to believe—was enabled by God's Holy Spirit to embrace the promise of divine forgiveness and salvation through Jesus' vicarious death.

Court of High Commission: a special legal court instituted by the Crown and charged with enforcing ecclesiastical laws and regulations of the Church of England.

covenant: literally an agreement between two parties similar to a contract. In Puritan thought, God assumed the primary role for upholding any covenant made with humankind. God's promises established an orderly framework for divine dealings with humankind.

Covenant of Grace: in Reformed theology, the promise of God to grant forgiveness, salvation, and eternal life through the sacrificial death of Jesus to those who embrace that promise in true faith.

Covenant of Works: in Reformed theology, the promise of God to humankind's first parents to provide eternal life on the condition that they obey the divine command to remain righteous by abstaining from the forbidden fruit. When Adam and Eve broke the covenant, eternal life could no longer be obtained through good works.

deacon: Greek *diakonos*, "one who serves." A church office focused on works of service. In the churches of Massachusetts Bay, the deacons assisted the elders and pastor by assisting with charities, maintaining order in services, distributing communion, and attending to the church's secular affairs.

elder: a lay church leader chosen by the congregation, usually by majority vote, to assist the pastor in administering the spiritual affairs of the congregation.

election: the Reformed doctrine that God chose particular people for salvation out of the mass of sinful humanity.

Elizabethan Settlement: The order of church government, doctrine, and ceremony established shortly after the accession of Elizabeth I to the throne of England. The government was episcopal. The doctrine was Protestant. The ceremonies, which were laid out in the Elizabethan Book of Common Prayer, expressed Protestant ideas but preserved many traditional forms inherited from Roman Catholicism. See also "*via media.*"

episcopal: a form of church government characterized by a hierarchy of authority. In England, the monarch was the head of the church and held ultimate power to appoint all officers. Monarchs appointed archbishops (England had two—York and Canterbury), who in turn appointed bishops over particular territories or dioceses. Bishops in turn appointed priests to serve particular local churches.

Eucharist: see "Lord's Supper." This name for communion emphasized joyful celebration.

faith: a key Christian concept which, in Protestantism, involves not merely belief in the sense of accepting *that* a God exists or that an idea or a promise is true, but in placing one's trust *in* that person, idea, or promise in the full expectation that the person will act or the promise will be fulfilled for the believer.

Familists: also known as the "Family of Love," it was a sixteenth-century sect founded by the Dutch visionary Hendrik Niclaes. Familists were reputed to teach that divine visions or personal revelations superseded the Bible and united the believer to Christ in such a way that they achieved a sinless perfection which liberated them from further obligation to the moral law.

free grace: the belief that God dispensed grace without condition, that a believer could do nothing to prepare for that grace and that a person's good works did not provide trustworthy evidence that the person had truly believed as one of the elect. Assurance that one was truly elect came from an inner sense placed directly within the believer by the Holy Spirit. See also "assurance."

godliness: the virtue of desiring to please God in all one's thoughts and behaviors, and of striving to fulfill those desires in one's practice.

godly: the term by which puritans most commonly identified themselves as a movement of people dedicated to cultivating godliness in personal and church life.

heresy, heretical: Greek *hairesis*, "philosophical school or teaching." Teaching about God, theology, and spiritual life which conflicts with or directly contradicts accepted Church teaching (see "orthodox").

indulgences: special pardons said to reduce the time a departed Christian had to spend in Purgatory before being admitted to heaven.

Traveling clergymen sold indulgences by the thousands in the sixteenth century to raise money for massive building projects in Rome. The printed forms had blank spaces where the seller could insert a name and the number of years' pardon a buyer had purchased for himself or a departed loved one.

John of Leyden: the sixteenth-century Dutch leader of a sect of Anabaptists who took over government of the city of Muenster. Leyden was crowned king and instituted a community of goods and the practice of polygamy for some months, until a combined force of Protestants and Catholics put down the rebellion.

justification: the divine act of making a believer right with God. Catholics and Protestants differed on how this was achieved. Catholics taught that justification was infused into the life of a believer through participation in the sacraments of the Church. Protestants beginning with Luther insisted it came when God declared the person righteous in the moment that person exercised true faith.

lay, layperson, lay leader: from the Greek *laos*, "people." Any member of a church who is not ordained as a clergy person. See also "clergy," "ordain, ordination."

Lord's Supper: the ceremony commemorating the salvation won for humans in sacrificial death of Jesus, expressed in eating bread (symbolic of Jesus' tortured and mortally wounded body), and drinking wine (symbolizing his shed blood). Protestants named the Lord's Supper as one of two "sacraments" or signs and seals of divine grace. See also "sacrament."

Luther, Martin (1483–1546): Universally regarded as the father of the Protestant Reformation. Luther attracted almost instant fame in 1517 when he posted on the church door in Wittenburg, Germany, his "Ninety-Five Theses" criticizing official Roman Catholic teaching. Luther's criticism of church abuses, his insistence on the doctrine of justification by faith alone, and his emphasis on the primacy of the Bible as the source of true doctrine became hallmarks of the Protestant Reformation.

means of grace: practices which puritans believed God had appointed to enable people to experience the grace of faith, forgiveness, salvation, and relationship with God. These included individual and communal prayer, reading of the Bible, listening to sermons, and participating in the sacraments of baptism and the Lord's Supper.

Muenster: a city in western Germany made famous in Protestant lore by a sixteenth-century Anabaptist revolt led by John of Leyden. Muenster became a trope in seventeenth-century Protestant writing for the threat of fanatical social disorder. See "John of Leyden."

nonconformer, nonconformity: a minister or layperson who refused from conviction to observe certain prescribed ceremonies, forms of worship, and regulations of the Church of England. See also "conformer, conformity."

ordain, ordination: an official conferring upon someone the office of priest or clergyperson, which gave that person the authority to perform certain duties reserved to that office such as preaching and administering the sacraments.

orthodox, orthodoxy: from the Greek *ortho*, "straight," and *doxa*, "opinion." Belief and teaching consistent with that accepted by the Church as expressed in its creeds and confessions, or summaries of church doctrine. Protestants insist that these creeds and confessions in turn must derive from Scripture as the sole authority in matters of religious faith and practice.

prayer book: see "Book of Common Prayer."

predestination: the doctrine that God chose or destined a person for salvation "before the world began." Different theological traditions offer different explanations of this doctrine, but Reformed Christians teach that God made this choice solely for God's own glory, without reference to any merit the person might have or knowledge of the person's disposition to belief or disbelief.

presbyterian: a form of church government characterized by a plurality of leadership in the local churches through elders or "presbyters," including the pastor and elected lay elders, along with oversight of all churches within a given district by a "presbytery," body of elders selected from each of the churches within that district. Presbyteries were further organized into several "synods" and the whole church into a "General Assembly," with plural representatives from each church sharing ruling authority at every level.

Reformed: the branch of Protestantism developed by a group of French, Swiss, German, and Dutch Reformers whose leaders included John Calvin, Heinrich Bullinger, and Ulrich Zwingli. Reformed Protestants stress divine sovereignty. They typically seek to bring Christian belief and practice into radical conformity with the Bible, insisting on eradicating any practice, form, or ceremony not explicitly sanctioned by Scripture.

resurrection: the Christian belief that at the end of time, the remains of the dead will be raised through reuniting of soul and body. True believers will enter body and soul into eternal life with God, while the unredeemed will be sentenced soul and body to eternal torment, the "second death." Christians believe that the resurrection of Jesus on the third day after his death not only validated his redemptive mission and ratified his identity as Messiah, but constituted the first instance of this general end-time resurrection.

Sabbath: for puritans, Sunday, the day of Christian worship, believed to continue the Old Testament Sabbath (from the Hebrew "seventh") day of rest and devotion to God. Puritans believed that the day had changed from the seventh day of the week to the first to commemorate the resurrection of Jesus from the dead, but the command to keep the day holy remained in force.

sacrament: for Protestants, a ritual believed to have been introduced by Jesus himself which symbolized central spiritual truths of the Christian faith. Reformed Christians defined a sacrament as a "sign and seal of grace." Protestants agreed there were only two: Baptism and the Lord's Supper, or Communion.

sanctification: the process of being set apart to God in a person's desires, beliefs, and behaviors. Puritans saw this as the work of God's Holy Spirit, not the results of human effort. Nevertheless, most believed that good works and godly practices could provide evidence that sanctification was taking place in a believer's life.

sanctificationist: the belief of many Massachusetts Puritans that good works and godly practices and disciplines could provide evidence that a person was one of the elect who had responded to God in true faith.

sermon-gadding: the puritan pastime of traveling to a neighboring village or town to listen to a sermon or lecture delivered by a visiting preacher. Often frowned upon and prohibited by bishops and parish clergy.

theology: the study of God and God's ways.

Thirty-Nine Articles: the articles which expressed the core Protestant teaching of the Church of England.

unorthodox: belief in conflict with accepted Church teaching (see "orthodox, orthodoxy").

vestments: ceremonial robes designed for wear by clergy while conducting worship services, especially services surrounding the celebration of the Eucharist.

via media: the "middle way" of worship and belief developed by Queen Elizabeth I and her bishops, which sought to win support of most English people by adopting core Protestant teachings while carrying over from Roman Catholicism many traditional ceremonies and forms of worship. See also "Elizabethan Settlement."

witness of the Spirit: an inner sense of confidence, peace, or assurance based upon promises of God drawn from specific Bible passages. The sense of confidence came as the believer embraced the promise as true in itself and as truly descriptive of what God had done spiritually within her or him. Puritans believed that the God's Holy Spirit gave this inner sense of confidence directly to a believer's soul. They differed over whether every believer would experience such a witness, or whether such a witness was required for true assurance. See "assurance."

works righteousness: the English Protestant term for the belief that good works could make a person right with God and worthy of salvation. Protestants rejected this idea, insisting that faith alone could save and make one right with God.

Study and Discussion Questions

Chapter One

1. How did Protestant ideas about salvation differ from Roman Catholic ones?

2. Why did Protestant leaders translate the Bible into spoken languages? What difference did that make in the way Protestants practiced their faith?

3. What was the Elizabethan Settlement or *via media*? What did people like Anne Marbury's father think of it?

4. What was it like for Anne Marbury to grow up in a godly family? How was it similar to the upbringing of other English girls? How did it differ?

5. What were the "means of grace?"

6. What did Protestants believe about women's roles? How did that compare with Catholic belief, according to historians?

7. What sorts of activities were available to godly English youth? How did they adapt these activities to pursue social interests?

Chapter Two

1. Describe the impact of James I's ascendance to the English throne upon the seventeenth-century English religious and commercial scene.

2. How did John Cotton's ministry at St. Boltoph's illustrate the choices a puritan faced under James I's bishops?

3. Describe the process of conversion.

4. Describe the two different ways puritans thought a person could receive assurance that their conversion was real. Which did Cotton believe?

5. What were some of the teachings which Anne Hutchinson's future critic Thomas Shepard dabbled in during his youth? Why did most puritans oppose these ideas?

6. What did anti-Calvinist priests and bishops such as William Laud believe about Church of England ceremonies? How did their beliefs shape their actions toward puritans?

7. How did colonization figure into the puritan response to Laud's program?

8. How did the decision to recruit *families* shape the society of early colonial Massachusetts? How did Massachusetts Bay differ from other English colonies as a result?

9. In what settings did the founders of Massachusetts Bay recruit most heavily?

10. How does Hutchinson and William Hutchinson's family illustrate the complex relationship between economic and religious motivations for moving to New England?

Chapter Three

1. How did the move to Massachusetts Bay help to make puritans aware of their differences?

2. What issues confronted early colonists about church organization and how did they resolve them? What was "congregationalism?"

3. What was a "church covenant?" Why did members sign it?

4. Why were Hutchinson and William Hutchinson welcomed to Boston? What resources did they add to the community?

5. What concerns were raised about Hutchinson at her membership interview and how were they resolved? What does this suggest about the religious tone in Boston in 1634?

6. What was the "culture of discipline" in early New England? How did authorities try to discourage bad behavior? How did they seek to promote good?

7. How did Anne Hutchinson promote the "culture of discipline" in early New England? How did William's offices involve him in promoting it?

8. What opportunities did Hutchinson's skills as healer and assistant midwife afford for building community among Boston women? For spreading her views on assurance? How did John Cotton feel about Hutchinson's activities?

9. How did the community respond initially to Hutchinson's spiritual leadership?

Chapter Four

1. As you read this chapter, keep track of reasons why the "old familiar story" spawned by Deputy Governor Dudley's remarks is "a bit too neat."

2. Who were the three new arrivals to the colony in 1635–1636 who contributed to the formation of factions? How did Sir Henry Vane contribute?

3. How did Anne Hutchinson's household meetings begin? What precedents existed for the formation of such meetings? How were they initially viewed by the colonists and leadership of Massachusetts Bay?

4. What evidence exists that Hutchinson may not have discussed everything she was later accused of discussing during her household meetings?

5. How did Thomas Shepard view the free grace ideas he encountered when he came to Massachusetts Bay? Why did he view them this way? Whom did he blame for the spread of these ideas?

6. How did Shepard's views on conversion shape the requirements for church membership in Massachusetts Bay?

7. What did Hutchinson's brother-in-law John Wheelwright contribute to the growing divisions in Boston?

8. How did Anne Hutchinson herself contribute to the development of the free grace faction in Boston? How did she likely view her own activities?

9. What event precipitated the outbreak of division in the Boston church? Why?

10. What did Hutchinson say at the "private conference" between her and the ministers in October 1636? Why might her words have offended the ministers?

11. Why did Winthrop oppose Wheelwright's ordination after he had "given satisfaction" to the ministers during the October conference?

Chapter Five

1. What other safety concerns did the Massachusetts Bay leaders have in 1636? How might their concerns about external threats have affected their views on the internal unrest within the colony?

2. If news of colonial discord reached authorities in London, how might they have reacted? What would have been the consequences for the leadership of Massachusetts Bay? For the religious life of the colony?

3. Why did Massachusetts Bay leaders call a public fast?

4. What effect did Anne Hutchinson's household meetings have on the controversy in Boston?

5. Why did Pastor John Wilson lose the support of his Boston congregation?

6. Why did John Wheelwright's Fast Day Sermon fail to heal the breach among the colonists?

7. How did Hutchinson's teaching in her weekly meetings contribute to the unrest in Boston and other towns of Massachusetts Bay?

8. What sorts of actions contributed to the divisions in Boston? Which actions were performed by men? Which by women? How did Hutchinson's own activities illustrate specific female tactics of leadership during this period?

9. Why did the General Court censure John Wheelwright at its February meeting? What does this suggest about the majority opinion in the colony at this time? Why did the majority vote to move the May meeting of the Court to Newtown?

10. Why did Sir Henry Vane lose the May election to the governorship? How did he and his supporters respond?

11. Why did the General Court treat Wheelwright as it did during its May session rather than sentencing him? Why did it not have the desired effect?

Chapter Six

1. What were the General Court's and Anne Hutchinson's respective agendas for her trial? What was "reduction," and how did John Winthrop expect to achieve it for Hutchinson? How did Hutchinson plan to defend herself?

2. Why did Winthrop organize a ministerial conference and synod before putting Hutchinson and her allies on trial?

3. Why did Hutchinson's allies jump to a defense of so many of the "erroneous opinions" drawn up by the ministers at their conference? What effect did this have on John Cotton?

4. What was the outcome of the ministerial conference and synod? How did the synod attempt to distinguish between Hutchinson's meetings and other meetings in private homes?

5. How did Anne Hutchinson and her allies respond to the actions of the synod? Why do you think John Cotton was not more forceful in enforcing the Synod's pronouncements?

6. Why were Hutchinson and John Cotton so concerned about Mary Dyer's stillborn baby? Do you think it was a good idea for them to conceal the news? Why or why not?

7. Why did John Winthrop and the General Court act against the male leaders of the free grace faction before summoning Hutchinson?

8. Why did Hutchinson reply to Winthrop's indictment by stating that she heard "no things laid to her charge?" How did this reveal her defense strategy?

9. How did Hutchinson refute each of Winthrop's first two charges—that she "countenanced those that are parties" in the petition drive for Wheelwright and that she held unlawful meetings in her home? Why did her refutations succeed in each case?

10. How did the accusation of Deputy Governor Thomas Dudley, that Hutchinson had "disparaged all our ministers," shift the momentum of the trial? Why did it matter so much what she said about the ministers?

11. How did Hutchinson's defense strategy work against the ministers' accusations that she had accused them of preaching a covenant of works? Did she ever deny that she did so? If not, how might her strategy have helped her? Why didn't Cotton's, Leverett's, and Cogshall's testimonies help?

12. What specifically did the General Court find so disturbing about Anne Hutchinson's claim to hear the voice of God's Spirit to her soul? What was the bigger problem, the claim itself or her prophecy that the General Court would be destroyed?

13. Why was Anne Hutchinson banished from Massachusetts Bay?

Chapter Seven

1. What was the initial response of the Boston community to Anne Hutchinson's sentence of banishment? Why?

2. As you read, keep track of Hutchinson's relationship with John Cotton. When do you think Cotton finally gave up on her? Why did he do so?

3. Why did the leaders of the Boston church decide to put Hutchinson on trial? How did the church trial differ from the civil trial? What was its purpose?

4. Why did Hutchinson's privacy defense fail so quickly in her church trial when it had given her so much mileage in the civil trial?

5. What does Anne Hutchinson's defense at her church trial reveal about seventeenth-century habits of reading the Bible? Why did the ministers challenge her way of reading certain texts? How did they decide which reading was the correct one?

6. Judging by Hutchinson's response to the connection Peter Bulkeley made between her beliefs on the Resurrection and Familism, do you think that Hutchinson intentionally held Familist or "libertine" views?

7. Deputy Governor Thomas Dudley hinted that Hutchinson did not write her own confessions and retractions, but that they had been dictated or even written for her by John Cotton and John Davenport. What do you think of this argument? Were Hutchinson's confessions sincere expressions of her repentance or not? If not, what might her motivation have been for stating them?

8. What, in Hutchinson's mind, was the distinction between an "error" and a "mistake?" Why did Cotton not accept her distinction, but charged her with "making a Lye?"

9. In what sense did Hutchinson act as a "husband rather than wife . . . preacher rather than hearer . . . magistrate rather than subject?"

10. Why did Winthrop keep track of Anne Hutchinson's activities after she left Boston?

11. Why did John Cotton treat the news about Anne Hutchinson's "monstrous birth" in Rhode Island so differently from his handling of the Mary Dyer case two years before?

12. Why did the community at Aquidneck fall apart so quickly?

13. Why did Thomas Weld interpret the significance of Hutchinson's death as he did?

Epilogue

1. How did *Mercurius Americanus's* view of Anne Hutchinson differ from that of John Winthrop and Thomas Weld? How did the author account for the difference?

2. Who do you think was the real Anne Hutchinson, judging from the evidence you have reviewed in this text?

3. Why do you think the figure of Anne Hutchinson has remained so fascinating to Americans throughout the centuries since her death?

A Note on the Sources

The full range of primary sources concerning Anne Hutchinson have long been unearthed and are widely available in published form. Those bearing most directly upon her life and trials have been collected in one volume edited by David D. Hall under the title *The Antinomian Controversy, 1636–1638: A Documentary History*, now in its second edition (1990). The edition includes the whole of John Winthrop's *Short Story of the Rise, Reign and Ruin of the Antinomians, Familists, and Libertines*, John Wheelwright's incendiary Fast Day Sermon, the full transcripts of her civil and church trials, and John Cotton's *Way of the Congregationalist Churches Cleared*, along with a number of other related documents. John Winthrop's private journal provides a second important source of information about Hutchinson and is available in a definitive edition, *The Journal of John Winthrop, 1630–1649*, edited by Richard Dunn, James Savage, and Laetitia Yeandle (1996). See also Allyn B. Forbes, ed., *The Winthrop Papers*, 5 vols. (1929–1947). The lively exchange between Hutchinson's father Francis Marbury and Bishop Aylmer is reprinted along with his petition to Sir William Cecil, Lord Burghley and his ordination certificate in the *Proceedings of the Massachusetts Historical Society* 48 (1914–1915), 280–290. Several of Hutchinson's brother-in-law John Wheelwright's principal writings concerning the period have been collected in *John Wheelwright: His Writings*, edited by Charles H. Bell (1970). Hutchinson's beloved teacher John Cotton's correspondence has been collected in *The Correspondence of John Cotton*, edited by Sargent Bush, Jr. (2001), and several of his relevant writings on the events of the 1630s appear in *John Cotton on the Churches of New England*, edited by Larzer Ziff (1968). A sample of his theology of intimacy with God and the Witness of the Spirit is available in a modern facsimile reprint edition of his *A Brief Exposition*, *with Practical Observations, upon the Whole Book of Canticles* (1972). *The Records of the First Church in Boston 1730–1868*, edited by Richard D. Pierce (1961), includes brief entries of those accepted for membership as well as those disciplined and excommunicated during the 1630s. Modern editions of relevant works of Hutchinson's nemesis, Thomas Shepard, include *God's Plot: Puritan Spirituality in Thomas Shepard's Cambridge*, edited by Michael McGiffert (1994), *Thomas Shepard's Confessions*, edited by George Selement and Bruce C. Woolley (1981), and *The Works of Thomas Shepard, First Pastor of the First Church, Cambridge, with a Memoir of His Life and Character* (1967). Writings and papers of others early settlers are available in a wide range of publications, including the *Collections* and *Proceedings* of the Massachusetts Historical Society, the *Publications* of the Colonial Society of Massachusetts, the *Proceedings* of the American Antiquarian Society, the *Publications* of the Narragansett Club, and the *Publications* of the Prince Society. Biblical quotations in the text are taken primarily from the Geneva Bible, which is available in several reprint facsimile editions, including *The Geneva Bible: A facsimile of the 1560 Edition*, introduction Lloyd E. Berry (1969), and *The Geneva Bible: The Annotated New Testament 1602 Edition*, edited by Gerald T. Sheppard (1989). The Authorized or King James Version was also quoted where noted.

Secondary Works

Anne Hutchinson has hardly suffered from historical neglect in the centuries since her exile and death. The most recent and by far the most theologically sensitive and informed interpretation of Hutchinson and her role in the free grace controversy is Michael P. Winship's *Making Heretics: Militant Protestantism and Free Grace in Massachusetts, 1636–1641* (2002), along with his more distilled treatment of her story in *The Times and Trials of Anne Hutchinson: Puritans Divided* (2005). A number of other scholarly works offer extensive treatment of Hutchinson in her times. Emery Battis's *Saints and Sectaries: Anne Hutchinson and the Antinomian Controversy in the Massachusetts Bay Colony* (1962), provides a lively account of the period, but is flawed by the unfortunate thesis that Hutchinson's misfortunes stemmed from psychological strains imposed by menopause and her weak husband. Darren Staloff's *The Making of an American Thinking Class: Intellectuals and Intelligentsia in Puritan Massachusetts* (1998) and Louise A. Breen, *Transgressing the Bounds: Subversive Enterprises among the Puritan Elite* (2001) argue that Hutchinson's ordeal served as the vehicle for a larger struggle over competing economic visions of early Massachusetts. Most studies of Anne Hutchinson, however, focus on gender. Leading works in this area include Jane Kamensky's *Governing the Tongue: The Politics of Speech in Early New England* (1997) and Mary Beth Norton, *Founding Mothers and Fathers: Gendered Power and the Forming of American Society* (1996). Hutchinson's biographers commonly take this perspective as well: see, for example, Eve LaPlante, *American Jezebel: The Uncommon Life of Anne Hutchinson, the Woman Who Defied the Puritans* (2004); Selma R. Williams, *Divine Rebel: The Life of Anne Marbury Hutchinson* (1981); and Helen Augur, *An American Jezebel: the Life of Anne Hutchinson* (1930).

Chapters 1 and 2

For excellent recent surveys of Elizabethan and Stuart England, respectively, see Patrick Collinson, *Elizabeth I* (2007); Penry Williams, *The Later Tudors: England, 1547–1603* (1995); and Mark Kishlansky, *A Monarchy Transformed: Britain 1603–1714* (1996).

The essential starting point for understanding the English Reformation is Eamon Duffy's *The Stripping of the Altars: Traditional Religion in England 1400–1580* 2nd ed. (2005). Patrick Collinson and Peter Lake have re-shaped the scholarship on Elizabethan Protestantism. See Collinson, *The Reformation: A History* (2004); *Godly People: Essays on English Protestantism and Puritanism* (1983); and *The Religion of Protestants: The Church in English Society 1559–1625* (1982). Also helpful for Elizabethan Puritanism is Peter Lake, *Moderate Puritans and the Elizabethan Church* (1982), as are several of the essays in Christopher Durston and Jacqueline Eales, eds., *The Culture of English Puritanism, 1560–1700* (1996). For a general overview of women's experience in early modern Europe, see Merry E. Wiesner, *Women and Gender in Early Modern Europe*, 2nd ed. (2000).

The historiography of women's experience in early modern England has grown especially rich in the past two decades. For a comprehensive overview, see Sara Mendelson and Patricia Crawford, *Women in Early Modern England 1550–1720* (1998). James Daybell's *Women Letter Writers in Tudor England* (2006) provides helpful insights into the growth and influence of literacy among women in this period. For marriage, see Diana O'Hara, *Courtship and Constraint: Rethinking the Making of Marriage in Tudor England* (2000). For family life, see Ralph A. Houlbrook, *The English Family, 1450–1700* (1984). For the influence of religion on women and family life, see Patricia Crawford, *Women and Religion in England 1500–1720* (1993) and Diane Watt, *Secretaries of God: Women Prophets in Late Medieval and Early Modern England* (1997). For the influence of Protestantism on marriage, see Anthony Fletcher, "The Protestant Idea of Marriage in Early Modern England," in *Religion, Culture, and Society in Early Modern England: Essays in Honour of Patrick Collinson*, eds. Anthony Fletcher and Peter Roberts (1994). For English midwifery, see Hilary Marland, ed., *The Art of Midwifery: Early Modern Midwives in Europe* (1993).

The accession of James I to the throne of England in 1603 marked a change of dynasty in England as well as a significant shift in the trajectory of English history. For essays examining its importance, see Glenn Burgess, Rowland Wymer, and Jason Lawrence, eds., *The Accession of James I: Historical and Cultural Consequences* (2006). For the significance of the Gunpowder Plot in English history, see J. A. Sharpe, *Remember, Remember, the Fifth of November: A Cultural History of Guy Fawkes Day* (2005). For the interaction of politics and religion under James I, see Kevin Sharpe and Peter Lake, eds., *Culture and Politics in Early Stuart England* (1993).

The relationship among preparation, conversion, assurance, and sanctification has received extensive analysis in many of the works listed here, but see especially Norman Pettit, *The Heart Prepared: Grace and Conversion in Puritan Spiritual Life*, 2nd ed. (1989); Patricia Caldwell, *The Puritan Conversion Narrative: The Beginnings of American Expression* (1983); R.T. Kendall, *Calvin and English Calvinism to 1649* (1979); Timothy D. Hall, "Assurance, Community, and the Puritan Self in the Antinomian Controversy, 1636–1638," in *Puritanism and Its Discontents*, ed. Laura Lunger Knoppers (2003).

The study of popular Protestantism and what has been called the "Puritan underground" in early Stuart England has flourished in the past two decades. A fascinating study is Peter Lake's *The Boxmaker's Revenge: "Orthodoxy," "Heterodoxy" and the Politics of the Parish in Early Stuart London* (2001). Other significant studies include Christopher W. Marsh, *The Family of Love in English Society, 1550–1630* (1994); and David R. Como, *Blown by the Spirit: Puritanism and the Emergence of an Antinomian Underground in Pre-Civil-War England* (2004). Most godly clergymen attempted to distance themselves from such movements and to correct them, as evidenced in Tom Webster's *Godly Clergy in Early Stuart England: The Caroline Puritan Movement, 1620–1643* (1997). For the Laudian reaction to godly Protestantism and Calvinism, see Nicholas Tyacke, *Anti-Calvinists: The Rise of English Arminianism, 1590–1640* (1987).

Biographies exist for several of Hutchinson's teachers, leaders, and opponents. Principal among these is Governor John Winthrop, the subject of an excellent critical biography by Francis J. Bremer, *John Winthrop: America's Forgotten Founding Father* (2003). Edmund S. Morgan's *The Puritan Dilemma: The Story of John Winthrop*, 3rd ed. (2007) has become the classic treatment. For John Cotton, see Larzer Ziff, *The Career of John Cotton: Puritanism and the American Experience* (1962). For John Wheelwright and Thomas Shepard, see the introductions to the collections of primary works listed above.

Chapters 3–5

The Great Migration to New England has remained a subject of intense scholarly interest over many decades. Two excellent studies are Virginia DeJohn Anderson, *New England's Generation: The Great Migration and the Formation of Society and Culture in the Seventeenth Century* (1991) and David Cressey, *Coming Over: Migration and Communication between England and New England in the Seventeenth Century* (1987). Darrett B. Rutman provides a detailed account of how the colonists founded the first communities during the early months after their arrival in Massachusetts Bay, and perceptive analysis of the development of seventeenth century Boston in *Winthrop's Boston: A Portrait of a Puritan Town, 1630–1649* (1965). Roger Thomson explores the extensive web of migratory connections between East Anglia and New England in *Mobility and Migration: East Anglian Founders of New England, 1629–1640* (1994). See also David Grayson Allen, *In English Ways: The Movement of Societies and the Transfer of Local Law and Custom to Massachusetts Bay in the Seventeenth Century* (1981).

For the transfer and adaptation of godly ideals to the New England setting, see Stephen Foster, *The Long Argument: English Puritanism and the Shaping of New England Culture, 1570–1700* (1991); and Francis J. Bremer, *The Puritan Experiment: New England Society from Bradford to Edwards*, 2nd ed. (1995). Edmund S. Morgan's *Visible Saints: The History of a Puritan Idea* (1963) analyzes the development of New England Congregationalism, while David D. Hall offers an interpretation of the development of the Congregational ministry in *The Faithful Shepherd: A History of the New England Ministry in the Seventeenth Century* (1972). Michael Winship examines the famous early unity of the Boston church in "'The Most Glorious Church in the World': The Unity of the Godly in Boston, Massachusetts, in the 1630s," *Journal of British Studies* 39 (2000), 71–98.

For an excellent brief overview of women's experience in early Massachusetts Bay, see Laurel Thatcher Ulrich, "John Winthrop's City of Women," *The Massachusetts Historical Review* 3 (2001), 19–48. For the role of godly religion in New England women's experience, see Amanda Porterfield, *Female Piety in New England: The Emergence of Religious Humanism* (1992), and early essays in Marilyn J. Westerkamp, ed., *Women and Religion in Early America, 1600–1850* (1999). For godly women's roles as spiritual guides and counselors, see Thomas Freeman, "'The Good Ministrye of Godlye and Vertuouse Women': The Elizabethan Martyrologists and the Female Supporters of the Marian Maryrs," *Journal of British Studies* 39 (2000), 8–33; Michael P. Winship, "Briget Cooke and the Art of Godly Female Self-Advancement," *Sixteenth Century Journal* 33 (2002), 1045–1054; and David R. Como, "Women, Prophecy, and Authority in Early Stuart Puritanism," *Huntington Library Quarterly* 61 (2000), 203–222. See also works by Mary Beth Norton and Jane Kamensky cited above.

Battis, *Saints and Sectaries*, provides the clearest and most engaging narrative of the beginnings of the "secret quarrels" and how they developed into full-blown factionalism by the summer of 1637, though Michael Winship offers very important correctives to in *Making Heretics* (both cited in full above). Janice Knight focuses on the disagreements between John Cotton and Thomas Shepard in her *Orthodoxies in Massachusetts: Rereading American Puritanism* (1994). The life of Sir Henry Vane is recounted in Violet A Rowe, *Sir Henry Vane the Younger: A Study in Political and Administrative History* (1970), while David Parnham analyzes the young firebrand's theological views in *Sir Henry Vane, Theologian: A Study in Seventeenth-Century Religious and Political Discourse* (1997). Philip F. Gura provides a broader analysis of gody "radicalism" in *A Glimpse of Sion's Glory: Puritan Radicalism in New England, 1620–1660* (1984). The development of the so-called Antinomian controversy is also treated in William K.B. Stoever, *A Faire and Easie Waye to Heaven: Covenant Theology and Antinomianism in Early Massachusetts* (1978), and Theodore Dwight Bozeman, *The Precianist Strain: Disciplinary Religion and Antinomian Backlash in Puritanism to 1638* (2004).

Chapters 6–7

Many of the works already cited contain extensive analysis of Hutchinson's trials, but see especially Winship, *Making Heretics* and *The Times and Trials of Anne Hutchinson*, and Mary Beth Norton, *Founding Mothers and Fathers*. This biography follows Winship in treating the case against Hutchinson as legitimate in seventeenth-century legal terms and coherent from start to finish, but it must be acknowledge that it is a minority view. Many earlier historians argued either that the case was trumped up by the Massachusetts authorities, or that it fell apart after John Cotton's testimony. For an example of the former view, see Ann Fairfax Withington and Jack Schwartz, "The Political Trial of Anne Hutchinson," *New England Quarterly* 51 (1978), 226–240; for the latter, see Edmund S. Morgan, "The Case against Anne Hutchinson," *New England Quarterly* 10 (1937), 635–649 as well as his chapter on Anne Hutchinson in *The Puritan Dilemma*. Michael G. Dittmore provides a close contextual analysis of Hutchinson's fateful "revelations" in "A Prophetess in Her Own Country: An Exegesis of Anne Hutchinson's 'Immediate Revelations,'" *William and Mary Quarterly* 3rd ser., 57 (2000), 349–392.

The evidence of Anne Hutchinson and her family in Rhode Island is extremely sketchy. Accounts of the founding of Rhode Island may be found in Sydney V. James, *Colonial Rhode Island: A History* (1978), as well as his *The Colonial Metamorphoses in Rhode Island: A Study of Institutions in Change* (2000). For Anne Hutchinson's "monstrous birth" see Anne Jacobson Schutte, "'Such Monstrous Births': A Neglected Aspect of the Antinomian Controversy," *Renaissance Quarterly* 38 (1985): 85–106; and Margaret V. Richardson and Arthur T. Hertig, "New England's First Recorded Hidatidiform Mole: A Historical Note," *New England Journal of Medicine* 260 (1959), 544–545. For Dutch-Amerindian relations, including the conflict in which Anne Hutchinson lost her life, see Donna Merwick, *The Shame and the Sorrow: Dutch-Amerindian Encounters in New Netherland* (Philadelphia: University of Pennsylvania Press, 2006).

Epilogue

Alternatives to John Winthrop's jaundiced interpretation of Anne Hutchinson's case are represented throughout this bibliographic essay. For an analysis of Anne Hutchinson's changing treatment as a symbol of American womanhood and dissent in the centuries since her death, see Amy Schrager Lang, *Prophetic Woman: Anne Hutchinson and the Problem of Dissent in the Literature of New England* (1987).

Index

Acts and Monuments (Foxe), 6
Adam, 128, 129
Adiaphora, 26–27
Admonition, 130, 131–132
Adultery, 54
Ahab (king), 16
Alford, 10, 11*f*, 22
Ananias, 136–137
Anger, 28
Anglicanism, 8
Antinomianism, 32, 68, 75–76, 143
Aquidneck Island, 137, 138*f*,
    142, 143
Arbella, 40
Arminius, James, 34
Aspinwall, William, 105–106,
    110–111
Assurance, 28, 29
    Cotton on, 30, 52, 71, 72, 77–78
    through good works, 29, 30, 57, 70,
        85–86, 90, 94
    of Hutchinson, A., 70
    in sanctification, 52, 77–78, 94, 96
    Shepard on, 69, 73
    Wilson, J., on, 52
Aylmer, John, 9

Bancroft, Richard, 25
Banishment
    Hutchinson, W., after, 123, 126, 143
    of Hutchinson, A., 1, 122, 124,
        125–126, 137, 139
    of Williams, 60–61, 139
Bartholomew, William, 49
Beacon Hill, 46

Bible, 3, 4
    Acts 26:16, 75
    Ecclesiastes 3:18–21, 128
    Ecclesiastes 12, 129
    Ephesians 2:8, 29
    Ezekiel 36:26, 73
    Geneva, 10, 14, 15
    Hebrews 4:12, 128
    Hebrews 9:16, 119
    Hebrews 13:5, 75
    I John 2:18, 119
    Isaiah, 22, 42
    John 13:35, 51
    John 16:12, 51
    King James Version, 25
    Matthew 18, 80
    midwifery in, 56
    New Testament, 14–15, 16, 47, 88,
        136–137
    Old Testament, 14–15, 16, 22
    in Protestant Reformation, 31
    Revelation 22:15, 135–136
    Romans 6:2–7, 129
    Song of Solomon, 90
    Thessalonians 5:23, 128
    Titus 2:3–5, 113–114
    translation of, 4–5, 6
Bilsby, 74
Bishops, 7, 25
Block Island, 84
Book of Canons, 25
Book of Common Prayer, 6, 7
    adiaphora in, 27
    catechism of, 14
    rituals in, 35

Boston, 27, 50f
  colonization of, 45–46
  Cotton in, 51
  harbor, 41f, 42
  Hutchinson family in, 49–50, 51
  religion in, 48
  Shepard on, 63
Bradstreet, Anne, 13, 49
Bradstreet, Simon, 66, 114–115
Brereley, Roger, 31–32, 33
Browne, Robert, 9
Bulkeley, Peter, 96, 104, 129–130

Calling, 15
Calvin, John, 5, 7
Calvinism, 7, 34–36
Catholicism, 3
  Laud's return to, 35, 36
  midwives in, 56
  Protestantism and, 5
  Roman, 4
Cecil, William, 12
Charity
  by Hutchinson, A., 44
  in New England, 55
Charles I (king), 23, 34
Charlestown, 45–46
Childbirth, 56
  deformity at, 108, 109, 140–141
  religion at, 57, 58
Church. *See also* Excommunication
  after New Testament, 142
  congregational model of, 48
  covenant, 48
  discipline by, 54–55
  membership in, 47, 48, 51–52, 69–70
  structure of, 46, 47–48
Church of England, 5
  Calvinism and, 34–36
Clarke, John, 140
Coddington, John, 105–106, 140, 142
Coddington, William, 49, 99, 102
Coggeshall, John, 77, 102, 105, 110, 118
Colburn, William, 102
Collins, Anne, 142, 143
Collins, William, 142, 143
Commission for Regulating Plantations, 84
Communion, 4, 35, 36
Concord, 95–96
Conventicles, 66

Conversion, 29
  narrative of, 69–70
  as requirement, 69–70
  Shepard's, 31–32
  sin after, 78
Cooke, Briget, 58
Cope, Anthony, 12
Corruption, 26
Cotton, John, 21, 22, 23, 125
  on assurance, 30, 52, 71, 72, 77–78
  in Boston, 51
  Concord and, 95–96
  on Dyer baby, 108–109
  emigration and, 100
  farewell sermon by, 40
  on free grace, 96, 98
  High Court summons of, 36
  Hutchinson, A., on, 115, 116, 117, 118, 119
  on Hutchinson, A., 58, 59, 62, 67, 69, 77, 79, 105, 121, 130–132, 133–134, 135–137, 140–141
  persecution of, 42
  questioning of, 70–74, 86
  sanctification of, 103–104
  Shepard and, 70–74
  on soul, 128
  at synod, 105–106
  at trial, 22, 136–137
  as vicar, 27–28
  Wilson, J., and, 88–89, 96
  Winthrop and, 51
  on women's protests, 92
Court of High Commission, 9, 35–36
Court of King's Bench, 84
Courtship, 20–21
Covenant of Grace. *See* Grace
Craddock, Matthew, 38
Crawford, Patricia, 17
Creature graces, 134
Cromwell, Oliver, 74
Culture of discipline, 53

D'Aulnay, Charles, 83
Davenport, John, 128–129, 132
Deborah, 16
Delilah, 16
Disease, 46
Disfranchisement, 54, 110–111
Dispensation, 12
Dittmore, Michael, 121
Domestic service, 18

Dryden, family of, 11–12
Dudley, Thomas, 45
   church covenant by, 48
   as governor, 51
   on Hutchinson, A., 62, 71, 134
   as magistrate, 55
   at trial, 62–63, 115, 116, 118, 120, 122, 134
   Winthrop's feud with, 65
Dumb dogs, 7
Durham House Group, 34
Dyer, Mary, 108, 109, 141
Dyer, William, 109

Easton, Nicholas, 141
Edward VI (king), 5
Election, 8, 13–14
   of Hutchinson, W., 53
   May, 97–100, 101
Election Day Sermon, 98
Eliot, John, 122, 133, 135
Elizabethan Settlement, 6, 9, 10
Elizabeth I (queen), 2, 5–6, 24
Emigration, 100, 103
Emmanuel College, 27, 31
Endicott, John, 60
England
   Church of, 5, 34–36
   as doomed, 37
   Navy of, 6
   Protestantism in, 5
Ephesians 2:8, 29
Episcopalianism, 7
Eve, 16
Excommunication, 54–55
   of Hutchinson, A., 126, 135, 136, 137, 141

Faith, 4, 7, 8, 13–14
Familists, 33, 71, 72, 73. See also Short Story of the Rise, Reign and Ruin of the Antinomians, Familists, and Libertines (Winthrop)
   on Resurrection, 127, 129–130, 131
Family, 10, 11. See also Individual families
   chores in, 17–18
   religion in, 12–13, 14, 15
"Family of Love," 33. See also Familists
Fast Day Sermon, 89–90, 91, 93–97, 110
Fasting, 19
Fawkes, Guy, 26

Fenwick, Anne, 58
Forgiveness, 3–4
Fort Saybrook, 84
Foxe, John, 6
Foxe's Book of Martyrs (Foxe), 6
Frederick V (king), 37
Free Grace, 63, 82, 95
   after Vane, Henry (the Younger), emigration, 103
   Cotton on, 96, 98
   Hutchinson, A., on, 51–52, 71, 79–80, 92–93, 99, 116, 119, 133
   sanctification and, 63–64, 85–86
   Synod, 104–108
   Wheelwright, J., views on, 30, 64, 74, 75, 78, 90, 106–107
   Wilson, J., and, 88
   Winthrop on, 96
Free love, 127, 130. See also Familists
Freemen, 53

Gender, 15–17. See also Women
   boundaries of, 112–113
   in New England, 39
"General Observations" (Winthrop), 44
Good works. See also Sanctification
   antinomianism and, 32
   assurance through, 29, 30, 57, 70, 85–86, 90, 94
Grace, covenant of, 14–15, 28, 89. See also free grace
Great Awakening, 2
Greater East Anglia, 11f
   economy of, 40
Great Migration, 40–41, 42
Greensmith, Stephen, 94
Griffin, 42
Gunpowder Plot, 26

Hampton Court Conference, 25
Hawkins, Jane, 56, 57
Hawthorne, Nathaniel, 2
Henrietta Maria, 36
Henry VIII (king), 5
Heresy, 5, 33, 103
Hett, Anne, 126
Higginson, Francis, 39
Holy Ghost, 77, 78, 79, 86, 141–142
Hooker, Thomas, 38, 69, 104, 108
Hutchinson, Anne
   accusations by, 77
   Admonition of, 130, 131–132

assurance of, 70
banishment of, 1, 122, 124, 125–126, 137, 139
charity work of, 44
church membership of, 51–52
confession by, 133–135
on Cotton, 115, 116, 117, 118, 119
Cotton on, 58, 59, 62, 67, 69, 77, 79, 105, 121, 130–132, 133–134, 135–137, 140–141
death of, 143
Dudley on, 62, 71, 134
excommunication of, 126, 135, 136, 137, 141
on free grace, 51–52, 71, 79–80, 92–93, 99, 116, 119, 133
as leader, 55–56, 62, 63, 65–68, 82–83, 86–88, 91, 92, 93, 100–101, 107–108, 112–115, 125, 136, 140, 141–142
as midwife, 56, 57, 58, 108–109
as mother, 57, 61, 140–141
Resurrection views of, 126–130, 131, 133
revelation of, 120–121, 122
Shepard on, 78–79, 132, 133, 135
in synod, 105
trials of, 1, 22–23, 43, 62–63, 81, 102–103, 111–121, 122, 126, 127–137
Weld on, 75–76, 134–135, 141, 143
Wheelwright, J., and, 57, 61, 67–68, 76–77, 81–82, 95, 111
Wilson, E., and, 92
Winthrop on, 58, 63, 66, 79, 82, 124, 136
Hutchinson, Edward, 126, 130, 142
Hutchinson, Francis, 142, 143
Hutchinson, John, 20
Hutchinson, Richard, 20, 142
Hutchinson, Samuel, 100
Hutchinson, Susanna, 143
Hutchinson, William, 20
after banishment, 123, 126, 143
business of, 41–42, 49, 53
death of, 143
election of, 53
as officeholder, 53–54, 59–60
Hutchinson, Zuriel, 61
Hutchinson family
in Boston, 49–50, 51
church membership of, 52

as freemen, 53
migration, 41–42, 142–143
size of, 51

Idolatry, 5
Indulgences, 3–4
Isaiah, 22, 42

James I (king)
assassination attempt on, 25–26
Calvinist support by, 34
as evil, 36–37
Protestantism under, 23, 24, 25, 26
Jennison, William, 122
Jesus
forgiveness from, 4
women and, 16
Jezebel (queen), 16
John of Leiden, 32–33
Johnson, Edward, 91
Johnson, Isaac, 48
Jones, John, 96

King's Privy Council, 84
Knollys, Hansard, 75

La Tour, Charles, 83
Laud, William, 34
as Catholic, 35, 36
Massachusetts Bay Company and, 85
Protestant Reformation and, 35–36
on sanctification, 85
Lay counseling, 58
Legal preachers, 95–96
Leisure, 18–19
Leverett, Thomas, 77, 79, 102
at trial, 118, 126, 132
Lincolnshire, 10, 11f
Literacy, 15
Luther, Martin, 3, 7

Marbury, Bridget, 10
Marbury, Francis, 6
death of, 21
family of, 10, 11–13, 14, 15, 17–18
puritanism of, 8–9, 10, 12–13
trial of, 8–9
Marriage
liberation from, 127
of priests, 5

under Protestant Reformation, 17
Resurrection and, 130
"Martin Marprelate" tracts, 12
Mary (queen), 5
Mass, 4
Massachusetts Bay Company, 23
charter of, 84, 101
colonization by, 37–40
dispersion of, 46
emigration from, 100
English control over, 84, 85
French traders and, 84
government of, 38, 44–45, 46,
48–49, 53, 54
Pequot War and, 84–85
population of, 58–59
price gouging in, 93
Protestantism in, 3
punishments in, 54
religion in, 38–39, 45, 46–48,
59–60
Mather, Richard, 70
McGiffert, Michael, 68
Middle way, 6
Midwifery, 18
in Bible, 56
in Catholicism, 56
of Hutchinson, A., 56, 57, 58,
108–109
licensing oaths of, 56
Millenary Petition, 25
Ministers
authority of, 47
ignorant, 7, 9
A Model of Christian Charity
(Winthrop), 40, 53–54
Mount Wollaston, 76–77, 80, 110, 139
Muenster, 32–33

Narragansett Bay, 143
Neile, Richard, 34
New England, 22, 23
charity in, 53
gender balance in, 39
New England Company, 37
New England Primer, 13
New England's Plantation
(Higginson), 39
New Hampshire, 139
Newport, 142
Newton, 97, 104–105
Newtown, 69

New World, 24. See also Massachusetts
Bay Company; New England
Niclaes, Hendrik, 33
Nineteenth Amendment, 2
Norton, Mary Beth, 113–114, 121, 136
Nowell, Increase, 119–120

Patriarchy, 17
Paul (saint), 16, 130
Pelham Bay, 143
Pequot War, 84–85, 99, 100–101
Perjury, 117–118
Peter, Hugh, 78, 88, 102
at trial, 115–116, 122, 135, 136
Phillip II (king), 6
Pilgrims, 9
Plymouth, 60, 137
Polygamy, 33
Pope, as Antichrist, 36–37
Popery, 6, 25
Portsmouth, 123, 139–140
Predestination, 7–8
Pregnancy, 56, 57
Prejudice, 117
Presbyterianism, 7
Preston, John, 31
Price gouging, 54, 93
Priests, 4
marriage of, 5
Promiscuity, 33
Prophesying, 60
Protestantism, 2
Catholicism and, 5
in England, 5
under James I, 23, 24, 25, 26
in Massachusetts Bay Company, 3
Protestant Reformation, 3
Bible in, 31
under Elizabeth I, 5–6
Laud and, 35–36
marriage under, 17
women during, 15–17
Punishment, 54
Purgatory, 3–4
Puritanism
literacy in, 15
of Marbury, 8–9, 10, 12–13
reputation of, 55
sermons, 19
women in, 16
for youth, 18–20
Puritan underground, 23, 42

Reduction, 102–103, 125–126
Religion
  in Boston, 48
  at childbirth, 57, 58
Religion (*Continued*)
  diversity in, 59–60
  in family, 12–13, 14, 15
  of Massachusetts Bay Company,
    38–39, 45, 46–48, 59–60
Remonstrance or Petition, 97, 110,
    124–125
Resurrection, 126–130, 131, 133
Revelation, 120–121, 122
Rhode Island, 137, 138*f*
Ritual, 4, 7
Rogers, John, 68
Roxbury, 124
Ruth, 16

Sabbath, 18, 54
Sacraments, 4
Salem, 45, 60
Salvation, 2–3
  through faith, 4, 7, 8, 13–14
  preparation for, 28, 31
Sanctification, 29–30
  as Antichristian, 90
  assurance in, 52, 77–78, 94, 96
  Cotton and, 103–104
  free grace and, 63–64, 85–86
  Laud on, 85
  Shepard and, 64, 69
  support for, 101
Satan, 97
Savage, Faith, 142
Savage, Thomas, 126, 130
Scotland, 24
Scripture, 121
Sedition, 95, 97, 110
Seekers, 142
Separatists, 9, 60
Sermon
  by Cotton, 40
  Election Day, 98
  Fast Day, 89–90, 91, 93–97, 110
  puritan, 19
  weekday, 59
Sermon-gadding, 19–20
Sex, 20–21, 54, 127, 130
Shepard, Thomas, 22, 23
  on assurance, 69, 73
  on Boston, 63

  career of, 68–69
  conversion of, 31–32
  Cotton's questioning by, 70–74
  Election Day Sermon by, 98
  as heresy hunter, 33–34
  on Hutchinson, A., 78–79, 132,
    133, 135
  Laud and, 36
  preaching by, 95
  as sanctificationist, 64, 69
  at trial, 22, 102, 125, 126, 127, 132,
    133, 135
*Short Story of the Rise, Reign and Ruin
    of the Antinomians, Familists,
    and Libertines* (Winthrop), 68,
    75–76, 143
Sin, 13
  after conversion, 78
  antinomianism and, 32
  confession of, 54
  freedom from, 28–29
Slavery, 101
Smith, John, 20
Sola scriptura, 31
Song of Solomon, 90
Soul, immortality of, 128–129
Spain, 6
St. Botolph's Church, 27, 28, 30
St. Martin in the Vintry, 18
Statue, 2
Stoughton, Israel, 118
Sunday, 18, 54
Symmes, Zechariah, 51–52, 126, 134
Synod, free grace, 104–108
Synod of Dordt, 34
Synods, 12

Theocratic despotism, 139–140
Thirty-Nine Articles, 6, 34
Thirty Years War, 37
Traducing, 118–119
Translation, of Bible, 4–5, 6
Transubstantiation, 36
Travel, 19
Trials
  of Hutchinson, A., 1, 22–23, 43,
    62–63, 81, 102–103, 111–121,
    122, 126, 127–137
  of Marbury, 8–9
  of Wheelwright, J., 94–95, 96–97,
    98, 99, 109, 110
Tudor, Mary, 40

Underhill, John, 84

Vane, Henry, 64
Vane, Henry (the Younger), 64–65, 85
  after Wheelwright petition,
    97, 98
  Concord and, 95–96
  emigration of, 100, 103
  on Wheelwright, J., 95
  on Wilson, J., 88, 89
Vestments, 35
Villiers, George, 34

Wecqueasgeeks, 143
Weld, Thomas, 68, 69, 85
  on Hutchinson, A., 75–76, 134–135,
    141, 143
  questioning of, 91–92
  at synod, 106
  at trial, 102, 134–135
  on women's protests, 92
Wheelwright, John, 22, 23
  Concord and, 95–96
  disfranchisement of, 110
  Fast Day Sermon by, 89–90, 91,
    93–97, 110
  free grace views of, 30, 64, 74, 75,
    78, 90, 106–107
  hiring of, 76–77, 79–80
  Hutchinson, A., and, 57, 61, 67–68,
    76–77, 81–82, 95, 111
  in New Hampshire, 139
  petition for, 97, 98, 109, 110
  at synod, 106–107
  trial of, 94–95, 96–97, 98, 99,
    109, 110
  Vane, Henry (the Younger), on, 95
  Winthrop on, 79–80
Wheelwright, Mary, 74, 139
Williams, Roger, 38, 142
  banishment of, 60–61, 139
Wilson, Elizabeth, 92
Wilson, John, 48, 77
  on assurance, 52
  baptism by, 51
  as chaplain, 99
  Cotton and, 88–89, 96
  free grace and, 88
  Hutchinson, A., dissent with, 82

  protest against, 92, 108
  on soul, 128
  at trial, 117, 134, 136, 137
Winship, Michael, 59, 64, 121
Winthrop, John
  church covenant by, 48
  on Cotton, 51
  Dudley's feud with, 65
  on Dyer baby, 108–109
  emigration enforcement by, 100
  on Fast Day Sermon, 91, 94, 110
  on free grace, 96
  "General Observations" by, 44
  on Hutchinson, A., 58, 63, 66, 79,
    82, 124, 136
  with Massachusetts Bay Company,
    24, 37–38, 46
  mercy by, 55
  A Model of Christian Charity by, 40,
    53–54
  on Pelham Bay, 143
  *Short Story of the Rise, Reign and
    Ruin of the Antinomians,
    Familists, and Libertines* by, 68,
    75–76, 143
  on soul, 128–129
  at synod, 104–105
  at trial, 1, 22, 43, 111–114, 116,
    118, 122, 132, 136, 137
  Vane, Henry (the Younger), and, 99
  on Wheelwright, J., 79–80, 110
  at Wheelwright petition, 97, 98
  Williams and, 60
Women
  chores of, 17–18
  clothing of, 60
  Jesus and, 16
  as lay counselors, 58
  meetings of, 16, 44, 62, 63, 64, 66,
    67, 68, 71, 74, 82, 86–87,
    112–115
  property of, 17
  during Protestant Reformation,
    15–17
  protests by, 92, 99, 108
  in puritanism, 16
  role of, 136
Women's Clubs, 2
Writing, 15